THE VEDA AND INDIAN CULTURE

The Veda and Indian Culture

An Introductory Essay

Kireet Joshi

MOTILAL BANARSIDASS PUBLISHERS
PRIVATE LIMITED • DELHI

First Published 1991
Reprint: Delhi, 1992, 1994, 2003

Published on behalf of
MAHARSHI SANDIPANI RASHTRIYA VEDA VIDYA PRATISHTHAN
UJJAIN-456 010 (M.P.)

ISBN: 81-208-0889-4

Also available at:
MOTILAL BANARSIDASS
41 U.A. Bungalow Road, Jawahar Nagar, Delhi 110 007
8 Mahalaxmi Chamber, 22 Bhulabhai Desai Road, Mumbai 400 026
236, 9th Main III Block, Jayanagar, Bangalore 560 011
120 Royapettah High Road, Mylapore, Chennai 600 004
Sanas Plaza, 1302 Baji Rao Road, Pune 411 002
8 Camac Street, Kolkata 700 017
Ashok Rajpath, Patna 800 004
Chowk, Varanasi 221 001

Printed in India
BY JAINENDRA PRAKASH JAIN AT SHRI JAINENDRA PRESS,
A-45 NARAINA, PHASE-I, NEW DELHI 110 028
AND PUBLISHED BY NARENDRA PRAKASH JAIN FOR
MOTILAL BANARSIDASS PUBLISHERS PRIVATE LIMITED,
BUNGALOW ROAD, DELHI 110 007

Preface

This brief book consists of a few reflections for beginners who are eager to understand the basic roots of Indian Culture and to explore the fundamental task of spiritual regeneration of contemporary India. This is an introductory essay, and it might serve as a stimulus to a growing number of youths who want to think seriously about our most ancient book of wisdom and its relevance to the present cultural needs. The attempt is to present some preliminary material for a rapid reading so that the readers might feel the need to study the subject of this essay in greater depth by taking recourse to authoritative works, particularly, those of Sri Aurobindo, such as *The Secret of the Veda*.

KIREET JOSHI

Contents

1

The Ancient Book of Wisdom

The age of Mysteries has come to be acknowledged as a common feature among some of the most ancient cultures of the world. Whether in India or in Chaldea, in Egypt or in Greece, in Atlantis or in some previously extant but now submerged islands of ancient times, there seemed to have flourished people with knowledge of secret truths. There was, undoubtedly, even a pre-Vedic age and a pre-Chaldean age, during which there seemed to have developed remarkable experiments and explorations leading to discoveries of momentous importance.

The results of these discoveries seem, however, to have been lost in some developments of the past, or they seem to have been assimilated—probably very much diminished in the content and import—in some traditions of religion or of philosophy. It is thus difficult to determine what exactly was the knowledge that the ancients possessed, and what exactly was their real achievement and their contribution to the advancement of mankind.

There is, however, available in India, the most ancient record, known as the Veda, a composition of a unique and accomplished character, the language of which is mysterious and ambiguous, betraying some possible secret. There is no doubt that the Veda preceded the Upanishads, which are themselves very ancient. There is no doubt also that the Veda speaks of *'pitarah'*, of the 'forefathers', and of their achievements in glorious terms. It seems, therefore, that we have in the Veda a record of some very ancient times (supposedly of 10,000 B.C.or of 5,000 B.C.),which might give us a clue of at least the Indian age of mysteries, and it might help us also in imagining or inferring what might have been the mysteries known and practised in other parts of the world.

There are, of course, historians who would like to convince us that the ancient times were barbaric, and that it would be vain to look for 'knowledge' or 'wisdom' in the traditions or records of those barbaric times. They would, of course, grant that these barbarians had some kind of religion, but this religion, they would maintain, had no profundity in it. They treat the history of religion as a kind of a logical development, of a gradual refinement and clarity, starting from animism and spiritism and superstitious magic to the presentday universal religions of monotheism, or theism or of existentialism. They would refuse to grant that there could have ever been in those ancient times anything better than any animistic or spiritistic practices or beliefs, or anything better than fetishism, totemism or tribal polytheistic cults or traditions. According to them, a hierarchical and systematic polytheistic religion was itself a later development, parallel to the political developments of early nations. To find, therefore, among the ancient records beliefs comparable to civilized and developed notions of pantheism or deism or theism would be, according to them, an impossibility.

This interpretation is being proved to be inadequate as larger data are being increasingly brought to light. It is true that the very ancient man was a barbarian, an infra-rational being, dominated almost exclusively by the needs of the physical, unillumined impulses and a mentality subject to physical senses. But at the same time, it has now come to be accepted that the infra-rational man is not wholly infra-rational, and that even he has some kind of implicit reasoning and a more or less crude supra-rational element. And it is not unlikely that at a certain stage of development, the infra-rational age may arrive at a lofty order of civilization. It may have great intuitions of the meaning of general intention of life, admirable ideas of the arrangement of life, a harmonious, well-adapted durable and serviceable social system, and a religion which will not be without its profundity. It is true that in this stage, pure reason and pure spirituality would not govern the society or move large body of men, but they may come to be represented by individuals at first few, but growing in number in due course. This may well lead to an age of great mystics, if spirituality happens to predominate. These mystics may find an atmosphere and surroundings suitable for delving into the profund and still occult psychological possibilities of our nature. It is true, again, that the favorable circumstances may have great limitations, and that these mystics would not be able to influence any large or even a considerable number of people. Even, they may be required to keep their deeper discoveries secret and impart them only to a small number of initiates. But they may also succeed in providing some powerful clues through which the popular barbaric mind may have a possibility of getting admittance, under certain conditions of development, into some intimation of the secrets. In some such development, we may find mystics of profound knowledge existing and flourishing as a secret minority of initiates in the midst of an overwhelming population of the barbaric mentality. Some such thing seems to have happened in the pre-historic India. And as secrets of the Veda are now being studied and understood, we feel how the composers of the Veda constituted a minority of the initiates, and how still they were able to give a peculiarly and uniquely spiritual turn to the whole future trend of the civilization.

Admittedly, the ancient barbarians looked upon the universe with some kind of animistic or spiristic feeling. It is true that to him, the most important things were the phenomena of Nature, the sun, the moon, stars, day and night, rains and storms and lightnings. To him, the world seemed to be peopled by unseen powers and by the earthly animals and birds and creatures of various kinds. It is natural, therefore, that the wise one living in company of the barbarian, and wishing to keep a safe line of communication with him to express his own knowledge would speak of these phenomena of Nature. But he would speak of them in a symbolic way. This would happen more imperatively if the wise one knows that there is no fundamental contradiction between the *real* truths of the universe and the *apparent* manifestations of these truths through the physical phenomena of Nature. Some such thing again seems to have occurred in the age in which the Veda must have been composed.

There seem to be three main grounds on which we are led to conclude that the Veda contains a huge mine of wisdom. First of all, and this is the most fundamental ground, the Veda reveals its full consistent meaning, only when its language is interpreted through certain keywords, which are ambiguous, and while they mean something very ordinary, in one sense, they mean something very extraordinary in another sense. To take only one example, the word *go* means a cow, in one sense, but it also means light, in another sense. Now it is found that if the word *go* is interpreted to mean cow in the Veda, it serves well up to a certain point, but this interpretation breaks down at some most crucial points, and thus on this line of interpretation the Veda might seem to be incoherent, bizarre, or meaningless. But, if this word is understood in the sense of spiritual light, it fits in fully and consistently in all the varied contexts throughout the Veda. This is only one illustration, but it has been possible to show, as has been shown by Sri Aurobindo in his book *On the Veda,* that the Veda has a secret wisdom, and that this secret pertains to the realm of deeper truths of existence. Secondly, the Upanisads, which came after the Veda, and which are universally acknowledged to be records of deep knowledge, declare the sacredness of the Veda. The thinkers of the Upanishads refer to the Veda as the highest authority for their own sublime utterances. They quote the Vedic verses as supporting citations, stating 'this is the word which was spoken by the Rig Veda' *(tad esha richabhyukta).* Thirdly, the Veda has been regarded as the highest source of knowledge throughout the long history of Indian tradition, and the entire line of orthodox systems of philosophy refers to the Veda as the highest indisputable authority of knowledge and truth.

It is also noteworthy that the poets of the Vedic verse were described by themselves as the hearers of the truth *(kavayah satyasrutayah).* They did not look upon themselves as a sort of superior medicine-men and makers of hymn and incantations to robust and barbaric tribe, but as seers and thinkers, *rishi dhira.* They themselves announced that their utterances had secret meaning, and that they revealed their whole significance only to the seers *(kavaye nivachanani ninya vachamsi).* The poetical form, the poetical rhythm and the poetical word in which the Vedic knowledge has been expressed are themselves consummate, and it is evident that their excellence, their force and their beauty betray some high and sustained inspiration. If we read this poetry without any false presumptions, we shall find that it is a sacred poetry sublime and powerful in its words and images, though with another kind of language and imagination than we now prefer and appreciate. We find that it is deep and subtle in its psychological experience and that it is stirred by a moved soul of vision and utterance.

Let us take the following example, and try to hear it directly in its purity:

> States upon states are born, covering over covering awakens to knowledge: in the lap of the mother he wholly sees. They have called to him, getting a wide knowledge, they guard sleeplessly the strength, they have entered into the strong city. The peoples born on earth increase the luminous (force) of the son of the White Mother, he has gold on his neck, he is large of speech, he is as if by (the power of) this honey wine a seeker of plenty.He

> is like pleasant and desirable milk, he is a thing uncompanioned and is with the two who are companions and is as a heat that is the belly of plenty and is invincible and an overcomer of many. Play, O Ray, and manifest thyself. (*Rig. Veda*, V.19)

Or again in the succeeding hymn,—

> Those (flames) of thee, the forceful (godhead), that move not and are increased and puissant, uncling the hostility and crookedness of one who has another law. O Fire, we choose thee for our priest and the means of effectuation of our strength and in the sacrifices bringing the food of thy pleasure we call thee by the word . . . O god of perfect works, may we be for thee felicity, for the truth, revelling with rays, revelling with heroes.

And finally, let us take the bulk of the third hymn that follows couched in the ordinary symbols of the sacrifice:

> As the human* we set thee within us, as the human we kindle thee, O Flame, O Seer-Puissance, as the human offer sacrifice to the gods for the seeker of the godheads. O Flame, thou burnest in the human creature when thou art satisfied with his offerings; his ladles go to thee unceasingly, O perfect in thy birth, O presser out of the running richness. Thee all the gods with one heart of love made their envoy; O seer, men serve and adore thee in their sacrifices as the godhead. Let mortal man adore the Will, the divine, by sacrifice to the powers divine; but thou, O Brightness, shine out high-kindled; enter into the home of the Truth, enter into the home of the bliss.

That obviously is a mystic and symbolic poetry and that is the real Veda, which when disclosed with the right key reveals itself as the ancient book of wisdom.

But what exactly is the content of the wisdom in the Veda? To this important question we shall now turn next.

*The godhead descending into man assumes the veil of humanity. The god is eternally perfect, unborn, fixed in the Truth and Joy; descending, he is born in man, grows, gradually manifests his completeness, attains as if by battle and difficult progress to the Truth and Joy. Man is the thinker, the god is the eternal seer; but the Divine veils his seerhood in the forms of thought and life to assist the development of the mortal into immortality.

2

The Mystic Fire

Veda is fundamentally a record of experiences of intuition and revelation. These experiences are varied, and they belong to various stages of development and exploration. The Veda records not only the experiences of the poets who have composed the hymns of the Veda, but also the experiences of the ancestors *(pitarah, poorvajanah)*. Veda thus describes the knowledge contained in the pre-Vedic tradition as also the Vedic tradition proper.

Among the four Vedas (Rig Veda, Yajur Veda, Sama Veda, and Atharva Veda), the Rig Veda is pre-eminent. According to one tradition, Atharva Veda was a later addition. The Rig Veda consists of 10 Mandalas (parts) and each Mandala consists of a number of Suktas, and each one of the Suktas consists of a group of verses.

The largest number of hymns are addressed and related to *Agni*, the mystic fire. This fact is significant, and it provides the central key to the treasure of the Vedic knowledge. *Agni,* like many other Vedic terms, has many meanings. It means fire, it means aspiration, force of consciousness, an urge, mounting and burning askesis. As we study the Veda deeply, we find that *Agni* is not only a principle of physical fire, but it stands much more constantly and thoroughly for the psychological principle of Will-Force. The Vedic poets make it abundantly clear that they regard the whole universe vibrant with a secret Will-Force, of which physical fire is only one outer manifestation, which can be used as a symbol in an attempt to bring the physical mind nearer to a sense and feeling for something that is deeply and profoundly present and dynamic in the universe.

Agni, according to the Vedic knowledge, is also the force of evolution, which pushes always forward, and breaks the tenebrous layers of Inconscience (tamas) and Matter (annam) and delivers the pulsating Life-Force. It is that which causes growth, and which increases the power, and which forges and welds relations among vegetations, plants and herbs, and which pushes forward the greater forces of Intelligence, which forms and builds complex organizations in which Mind can be lodged and made to vibrate effectively so as to make the material form not only conscious but even self-conscious. *Agni* is in itself a conscious will that acts as intermediary between the physical world *(bhoor)* and the intermediate worlds *(bhoovar)* and the higher world *(swar)*. *Agni* is described also as the messenger, who has a free access to all, and can communicate the intended message to any destination.

The Vedic seers have discovered that *Agni* is not only an impersonal force of will or aspiration, it is also a being, a God, who presides over all the psychological activities that relate to will, force, action, energizing. *Agni* can be contacted, he can be approached, he can be invited, he can be made active within us and within the universe. The Veda describes through its hymns not only the nature of *Agni*, but provides the exact vibratory sounds by which a dynamic contact with God *Agni* can be established. For, according to the Vedic poets, a sound or a certain secret set of vibrations tunes exactly with the vibrations which are appropriate to the vibrations of invisible psychological forces and entities. The Veda provides these secret sets of vibrations. The very hymns, their sounds, their specific measures are themselves these secret sets of vibrations. They are the mantras, the inevitable rhythmic expressions bearing the vibratory sounds packed with forces of realizations. These mantras invoke the deity and give the knowledge by which one can submit in admiration and devotion to the deity.

Mantras are thus not only expressions of knowledge, but they are also vehicles of devotion. They are also vibratory forces of dynamism and action. They contain the secret methods of art of action. Thus, the mantras are a wide synthesis of Jnana Yoga, the Bhakti Yoga, Karma Yoga and Mantra Yoga.

Agni symbolizes also the inner and true soul or our psychic being. We find in the Veda several references to this symbolism. The Rig Veda speaks of 'the boy suppressed in secret cavern'. (V.2.1). There is also in the Rig Veda this cryptic description, 'The son of heaven by the body of the earth' (III.25.1). There are some other descriptions also: 'He is there in middle of his house' (I.70.2). 'He is as if life and the breath of our existence, he is as if our eternal child' (I.66.1). He is 'the shining king who was hidden from us' (I.23.14). In the following verse, the Rig Veda brings out more clearly its secret knowledge of the nature and function of the psychic being symbolized by *Agni:*

> Oh *Agni,* when Thou Art well borne by us Thou becomest the supreme growth and expansion of our being, all glory and beauty are in Thy desirable hue and Thy perfect vision. Oh Vastness, Thou art a multitude of riches spread out on every side. (*Rig Veda,* II.1.12.)

It is important to note that the knowledge concerning the soul was in later times obscured, and except in the Upanishads and in some rare descriptions of the later philosophical or spiritual records, we have mostly ambiguous, confusing or misleading statements on this subject. Some later philosophies like Buddhism or Illusionism look upon the soul as a conglomeration of tendencies and Karma, which ultimately have to be extinguished. For them there is no reality of the soul-entity. Some others look upon the soul as an entity constituted by desire and other elements mixed with evil, which need to be and which can be purged out by a process of purification leading to the soul-realization. Some others still look upon the soul as a mere static presence or a static witness. They do not consider the soul as a principle of growth or as a leader of evolution. Some philosophers have spoken of the soul as one with the Supreme, others have thought of it as eternally different from the Supreme. There are still others who consider the soul to be inconceivably at once different from and identical with the Supreme. Some philosophers speak of the soul as *Jiva* meaning individual that is cosmic in nature. Some others speak of the soul as a *Chaitya Purusha,* meaning the individual that individualizes our existence on the earth. There are thus various views, and often conflicting notions are stated together causing much confusion and obscurity. It is for this reason that it is important to underline the pregnant and cryptic statements that we get in the Veda on this subject and try to understand and experience this luminous knowledge.

Agni also represents in the Veda the warmth and heat which is the basis of supramental transmutation. In fact, the heat released by combustion and other chemical reactions as also by the greater energy liberated by nuclear fusions and fissions is only the physical translation of a fundamental spiritual phenomenon which the Vedic seers know quite well. *Agni* represents that fundamental spiritual phenomenon, viz.,the action of the spiritual Fire in Matter. 'Oh Fire', says the Vedic verse, 'other flames are only branches of Thy stock. . . . Oh *Agni*, Oh universal Godhead, Thou art the navel-knot of the earths and their inhabitants; all men born Thou controllest and supportest like a pillar. . . . Thou art the head of heaven and the navel of the earth. . . . Thou art the power that moves at work in the two worlds.' (I.59). Again, in another verse, we find the following invocation of *Agni* in these words: 'That splendor of Thee, Oh Fire, which is in heaven and in the earth and in the plants and in the waters, and by which Thou hast spread out the wide mid-air is a vivid ocean of light which sees with a Divine scene.' And in the fourth verse of the seventh Sukta of the third Mandala of the Rig Veda, we have this cryptic but deeply significant description of *Agni*: '*Agni* has entered earth and heaven as if they were one.'

It is to be noted that the Vedic seers seem to have known that it is Agni that welds the supreme light and matter, and it is, therefore, Agni which can lead by its penetration into the cells of the body ('by entering heaven and the earth as if they are one') to the transformation of body.

It is thus clear that *Agni* is recognized by the Vedic seers as of fundamental importance in man's journey. *Agni* is the aspiration, and as such it is the priest *(Purohita)* that kindles the fire of aspiration and initiates man's journey. *Agni* is the soul, that which guides from within and illumines the path of the journey. *Agni* is the all-pervading energy and heat in the earth and in the heaven and it has the secret power of uniting the light of the heaven and the heat of the matter. It is thus the secret power of physical transmutation.

At its highest *Agni* is not merely the heat or the energy, not merely the soul, not merely a God, it is an aspect of the Supreme God-head itself. Verily, it is one of the sacred Names of the Supreme Divine Himself.

It is this *Agni* that is invoked by the Vedic seers at the beginning of the journey, and throughout the journey. This is one of the deep secrets of the Vedic knowledge. 'Aspire first', the Veda reveals to us in effect, 'burn within, kindle the Fire daily and for ever. It is this aspiration that will bring the Response from the Supreme and will lead to the fulfillment and perfection.' This is the initial but all-comprehensive message of the Veda.

But what about the journey itself? To this we shall turn next.

3

The Human Journey

Agni is not only the fire of the sacrifice, the fire of the journey of life, the élan of evolution, but also it is its leader and priest (purohita). *Agni* leads man in his search of the Truth (satyam). It is he who connects man with the cosmic forces and with all the gods of the three worlds (triloka), of earth (bhur), mid-world (bhuvar) and heaven (swar). At the head of swar is Indra, the god of Illumined Intelligence. It is Indra who shows man the path to the still higher realms and to the Supreme Reality. He cannot be overpassed, says Indra himself, in a colloquy between him and Agastya, a Rishi, who is impatient to shoot beyond to the Supreme, but finds Indra obstructing his path. 'I am your friend', says Indra to Agastya, 'I am not obstructing your path, but I am here on the path to take you to the Supreme. Why do you not invite me to your sacrifice?' Indra complains. Agastya understands, he invites Indra, and accepts to be led by him. In this short colloquy,* we have a very meaningful description of one of the secret experiences recorded in the Vedas.

But before one can reach the Supreme or the Supreme Light, (Savitri), one has to cross the four Guardians, the four Kings guarding the light of the Truth. These are the four gods, Varuna, Mitra, Aryaman and Bhaga. They are to be embraced and to be fulfilled before they lead the seeker to his goal.

Varuna represents vastness, infinite wideness, limitlessness. The Truth that the Veda worships is infinite, it is spaceless and timeless and yet is all Space and Time. This truth cannot be possessed without the widest wideness in our consciousness and in our being. In narrowness and in divisions, truth cannot be caught, and it escapes from all limitations, from all angularities. The seeker of the Vedic knowledge is therefore asked to break all narrowness, all divisions, all oppositions, all conflicts. He has to learn to comprehend and to contain all, all without limits. He has to

**Rig Veda*, I-70.

grow in the wideness of Varuna, worship him and be as wide as he is. Varuna answers the seeker, helps him and liberates him into the wide spaces of infinite being and prepares him to perceive all the infinities of the Supreme Light. The consciousness of man is broken by the mighty invasion of Varuna, and Varuna is fulfilled in man, who ceases to be mere mental and consents to be supramental.

But this is not enough. Mitra, the lord of Harmony is also to be fulfilled. The seeker must learn the secret of relations, know the threads that bind each to all and all to each. He must learn to be the friend of all creatures, of all men, of all gods. With the wideness of Varuna, he must combine the harmony of Mitra; wideness and relationships are both to be mastered. The Supramental Light is wideness but not empty of contents or relations. Hence the necessity of the union of Varuna and Mitra. And the seeker must serve these two gods, fulfill them, embody them and grow into their image.

But even this is not enough. In all human endeavor, there is the stress and strain of effort. There is a struggle, and it is through struggle, through intense effort, that the narrowness is overpassed, that the conflicts are resolved, wideness is achieved, harmony is established. One must have therefore the capacity for the highest effort, the intensest *tapasya,* a perfect mastery over all that needs to be done. Aryaman is the god of this mastery. Through him the highest effort is accomplished. He is total endurance. Without this endurance, we are like the unbaked jar, which will be broken at the touch of the Supreme Light. It will not be able to hold the nectar of immortality. The jar, our instrument, our body, our entire being, has to be baked, baked fully by the heat and austerity of Aryaman. He has to be worshipped, he has to be possessed, he has to be fulfilled. He prepares us, along with Varuna and Mitra, for the possession of Supreme Light.

But there is still Bhaga to be fulfilled. The Supreme Light is joy and we must learn not only the intensest effort but also the highest degrees of enjoyment. We know ordinarily the enjoyment of pleasure of the vital and of the physical. Even at the lower level the intense pleasure becomes an excitement and our balance is lost. We are not able to bear the pressure of enjoyment. Not many know the enjoyment of thought and of perception and of intuition, of beauty, of love, of ecstasy. All these enjoyments are to be known, experienced, possessed and fulfilled. But there are higher and still higher enjoyments. The Supreme Reality itself is a supreme enjoyment. Bhaga represents this supreme enjoyment. He is the god who presides over enjoyments, who is the eternal aspect of the joy of the Divine. He is to be approached, and in unity with Varuna, Mitra and Aryaman, he has to be embodied.

In his upward journey, the seeker then proceeds to *Savitri,* the lord of the Supreme Light, the sun in which 'all the gods unyoke their horses', the supreme in which gods cease to be *entities* and become His *aspects.*

This marks the victory of the Aryan seeker. He is now in the very home of the gods *(swe dame).* This is the home of the Truth, the Right and the Vast *(satyam, ritam brihat).* This is the supramental Truth-Consciousness *(Sat-Chit).* It is that by which reality expresses itself, and in which expression, even the Idea-Expression, is the concrete body of the Truth itself. It may therefore be described as the Real-Idea.

The Vedic seers seem to speak of primary faculties of the 'Truth-Conscious' soul: They are Sight and Hearing, the direct operations of an inherent Knowledge describable as Truth-vision and Truth-audition. It is these operations which are reflected from far off in our human mentality by the faculties of revelation and inspiration. This truth-consciousness is comprehensive, knows all, because it is all. It knows all in its universality and also in every detail of particularity. Light is here one with Force, the vibrations of knowledge with the rhythm of the will and both are one, perfectly and without seeking, groping or effort, with the assured result.

It is in this consciousness that is contained the honey, the nectar of delight. It is this honey (madhu) which is packed in the chariot of the *Ashwins.* The Ashwins, the divine twins, are the physicians of the gods who heal by the pourings of this nectar. It is this honey, soma, that is drunk by the gods and it is this soma drunk by the human seekers that gives to them immortality *(amritam).*

This, in brief, is the basic human journey of the Aryan described in the Veda. But there is still a further secret of which the Veda speaks, the secret of a further journey which is described through cryptic and ambiguous phrases and through somewhat incomprehensible legends.

To this secret we shall turn next.

4

The Deeper Secret

There is in the Veda the legend of the Cow and of the Angirasa Rishis. This legend, if properly understood, brings out a deeper secret.

The legend is simple. The Cows have been lost and the Angirasa Rishis are in search of these lost Cows. The sacrifice is to be performed, and the Angirasas have to chant the true word, the *Mantra.* Indra of all the gods is invoked. Indra comes down to help with his thunderbolt in which enter the powers of all the gods. Indra is the hero and fighter, and the battle is waged against certain powers, the *Dasyus* and the *Panis. Sarama,* the heavenly hound runs forward and finds out the Cows in the cave of the Panis. Indra strong with the Some-wine and the Angirasas, the Rishis, who are his companions, follow the track, enter the cave or violently break open the strong places of the hill, defeat the *Panis* and drive upward the liberated herds. The conquest is effected, and although Indra has done it once for all in the type by means of the Angirasas, yet he repeats the type continually even in the present. He is constantly the seeker of the Cows, 'gaveshana', and the restorer of the stolen wealth.

There are several variations of this legend in the Veda. Sometimes there is no reference to Sarama or the Angirasas or the Panis. Sometimes Agni is referred to as the God who breaks up the dark cave and restores the lost radiances. Sometimes both Agni and Indra have been described as having joined together in the battle over the Cows. 'You two warred over the Cows, O Indra, O Agni.' (VI.60.2) Sometimes it is Agni and Soma who are referred to as having joined together in the battle. 'O Agni and Soma, that heroic might of yours was made conscient when you robbed Panis of the Cows.' (I.93.4). Sometimes the Ashwins also are credited with the same achievement. 'You two (Ashwins) open the doors of the strong pan full of the kine.' (VI.62.II). Brihaspati is, however, more frequently the hero of this victory. 'Brihaspati, coming first into birth from the great Light in the Supreme other, seven-mouthed, multiply-born, seven-rayed, dispelled the darknesses; he with his best that possesses *Stubha* and the *Rik* broke *Vala* into pieces by his cry. Shouting Brihaspati drove upwards the bright herds with speed the offering and they lowed in reply.' (IV.50.4&5). And again in VI.73.1&3 we have the following: 'Brihaspati who is the hill-breaker, the first born, the Angirasa. . . . Brihaspati conquered the treasure *(vanuni)*, great pens this god won full of the kine.' Sometimes the Maruts also are associated in this action. Pushan also (the Increaser, a form of the Sun-god) is invoked for the pursuit and recovery of the stolen cattle. 'Let Pushan follow after our kine, let him protect our war-steeds. . . . Pushan, go thou after the kine. . . . Let him drive back to us that which was lost.' (VI.54.5.6.10). And in the hymn of Madhuchhandas (I.II.5) we have this striking image that gives a clue to all the variations of the legend, while addressing Indra, 'Oh lord of the thunderbolt, thou didst uncover the hole of Vala of the Cows; the gods, unfearing, entered speeding (or putting forth their force) into thee.'

In order to understand the deeper secret of the Veda, this legend of the lost Cows and of the Angirasa Rishis seems to promise us a key. Now the important word that is used for the Cow is go. But the word 'go' has also another meaning, viz., light, and it is this meaning which gives us the clue. The legend of the lost Cow is really about the lost light. The Vedic Rishis seem to suggest that there has occurred in the world process an event whereby the spiritual light has become obscured or has become concealed, and that this event has a relationship with an action of Panis, the sons of darkness. This concealment of light does not amount to the cancellation of light. There is no destruction of light. But there is nonetheless an effective covering of light. This covering is the Night of Darkness, but there is in it a secret light, which is the cherished possession of the forces of darkness, described as Dasyus and Panis, of whom Vritra and Vala are the Chief leaders. This is the distinctive feature of the Vedic idea of evil and darkness. For in this view, evil and darkness have in their deepest profundities their own cure. It is true that according to the Veda, evil and darkness have to be combated, but the end of the combat is not merely the destruction of evil and darkness, but also the *recovery* and *manifestation* of the light which is concealed *in* them. In other words, the light is not only to be discovered and possessed at the supreme height, in Swar and in Surya Savitri. The discovery of the light in Surya Savitri is followed and completed by the discovery and uncovering of the light in the very depths of darkness, of Inconscient, *tamas.* It seems that the whole legend of the Angirasa Rishis, who are described in the Veda as *pitarah,* forefathers, is a parable of a momentous effort and war waged by them in their search of the light that is at the end of the tunnel of darkness. It has been affirmed through this legend that one meets in the process of this discovery an opposition from the armies of Vritra and Vala, but also help from the gods. The gods, according to this legend, can be invited by a sacrifice, which in its inner significance, means the kindling of the inner aspiration, Agni. Each god can be invoked by a specific word, a *Mantra,* and the gods, when activised by the power of the Mantra, operate effectively in a war with the forces of darkness. Gods are thus partners of men in their struggle and battle. This battle has not only an *upward* movement but also a *downward* movement. Every step of conquest presents a gate leading to a further and a darker depth, requiring a greater and intenser help of the gods.

Thus, there is in the Veda the affirmation of the possibility of the recovery of the Sun that is lying in the darkness. It is said that the Sun, 'that Truth', was the thing found by Indra and the Angirasa in the cave of the Panis. By the rending of their cave, the Veda declares, the herds of the divine dawn which are the rays of the Sun of Truth ascend the hill of being and the Sun itself ascends to the luminous upper ocean of the divine existence, led over it by the thinkers like a ship over the waters till it reaches its farther shore.

In simple terms, the light is one, it is the same everywhere. It is not merely there *above,* it is also here *below.* In fact, the distinction between the above and below is itself a false distinction. It is true that ignorance is an effective phenomenon, but it is also something which can be effectively destroyed, so that the light above and the light below are both realized as the one identical light. Spirit above is not the only light, Matter below is also that very light, and matter too can be pierced by which the light which is concealed in its bosom can be made manifest. This is the deep secret of the Veda, and it is that which is held as a promise for an eventual realization in the history of the earth.

5

Significance of the Upanishad

The Veda and the initiates who were admitted to the secret of the Veda represented a lofty and consummate achievement secured by means of an intense and rapid cultivation of intuitive and supra-rational capacities and faculties. But the general mass of people in the midst of which this great and surprising Vedic phenomenon took place were evidently primitive and infra-rational, dominated by the needs of the body and limited to the engrossing demands of the physical mind. What was important for this mass of people was the Vedic ritualism, its ceremonies and the institution of sacrifice. In due course of time, this ritualism grew and developed into an elaborate and complicated system. It over-burdened the inner core of the Vedic secret, and it became increasingly difficult to penetrate through the crust of the outer ceremonies and acts to reach the inner heart of the true and living Vedic knowledge.

The inner Vedic knowledge was a kind of a synthesis of the spiritual and the physical, and this provided a fine balance and a graded ladder connecting the material and spiritual poles of existence. In this scheme, the outer ritual and ceremonies reflected the sunshine of the highest and profundest spiritual knowledge, and thus they were not a mere artifice or a misleading or imprisoning super-structure. They provided, on the contrary, a meaningful gate of entry for the physical mind of man to undertake the long journey of a true and balanced spiritual-material culture. The great achievement of the Vedic period was indeed the marvellous training that it provided to the physical mentality to admit the impress upon it of the brilliant rays of the spiritual light and to look upon men and the universe as a symbol of some deeper realities intensely worthy of adoration and worship.

But there is in the constitution of man, between the two extreme poles of the spiritual and the material, a gradation of powers and faculties of the vital and mental with their multiple seekings, motivations and aspirations, and a time must come in the development of any human social aggregate when these intermediate seekings of the vital and the mental would assert themselves and demand for themselves a larger and larger room for their activities and their rule. During this time there would naturally occur a confusion and dis-balancement in the original synthesis and organization of life. This would also cause a crisis, and in this crisis, there would occur exaggerated claims of outer ritualism creating a sharp conflict between itself and the rushing seekings and claims of the vital and mental powers. In this period of conflict, the spiritual nucleus of the old synthetic knowledge would tend to be exiled or thrown into a remoter and remoter background, with a possibility even of its being forgotten. If we study the history of the ancient periods of the early civilizations of Chaldea, Egypt, Greece, we find that there did occur during such a critical period of their history an eclipse of the power and hold of the knowledge of the secret Mysteries of spiritual and occult knowledge. This eclipse proved there to be total, and even in Greece, where the light of the Mysteries continued for some time, through Pythagoras, Stoics, Plato and Neo-Platonists, there came about finally a cleavage between the old and the new and there arose a dominantly vital and mental civilization in which the knowledge of the old Mysteries hardly played any role.

A similar thing could have happened also in India. In fact, it almost happened. At a time it seemed as though the inner core of the Vedic knowledge would be lost for ever and that India would begin a career of an exclusive vital and mental civilization. But this loss was greatly prevented, because there arose during the transitional period a remarkable movement, the parallel of which is not to be found in the history of any other ancient civilisation. For there occurred in India at this critical period of transition an intense and pristine search among larger and larger circles of people to recover the inner core of the Vedic knowledge, not merely through the preservation of tradition but by a consuming zeal of a psychological and spiritual practice. And through some of the passages of the Upanishads, we have brief glimpses of the picture of that extraordinary stir and movement of spiritual enquiry and passion for the highest knowledge. These passages present to us the scenes of that period of transition. We find there the great sages sitting in their groves ready to test and teach the seeker. We find princes and learned Brahmins and rich nobles going about in search of knowledge. The king's son in this chariot is in search of the spiritual secret. We have here a moving description of the intensity of Satyakama, the illegitimate son of the servant girl, seeking any man who might carry in himself the thought of light and the word of revelation. We meet here the typical figurers and personalities like Janaka, the great king who was also accomplished in spiritual knowledge and action. We meet also Ajatashatru with a rich and subtle mind, the great teacher Raikwa, who was in his outward profession a cart-driver, and Yajnavalkya, master of worldly possessions and spiritual riches, who cast at last all his wealth behind to wander forth as a houseless ascetic. We hear of Krishna, son of Devaki, who heard a single word of the Rishi Ghora and knew at once the Eternal. We see the Ashramas, the courts of kings who were also spiritual discoverers and thinkers and the great sacrificial assemblies where the sages met and compared their knowledge. We see here how in this critical moment the soul of India was born and how arose this unparalleled stir and seeking that secured for India a new line of spiritual resurgence and provided to all the posterity an unfailing fountain of spiritual waters that have poured themselves into all lines of inquiry and expression, not only those of religion and philosophy but even of science, art, literature, architecture and polity.

If India stands as a unique spiritual civilisation and if India has been able to keep some illuminating light burning even in its darkest period of inertia and ignorance and prevented the collapse of this mighty and profound culture, it is because of the strong foundations that were laid in this remarkable period of the transition.

6

The Veda and Indian Culture

The aim of life that the people are inspired to pursue determines the fundamental direction of their culture. From this point of view, it is necessary to examine what exactly was the aim of life proposed by the Veda and how it influenced the direction of the Indian culture.

According to one view which has been held largely by the western scholars and their Indian disciples, India has been governed by four important ideas, namely, (a) that this world is a constant flux *(samsara),* (b) that there is no substantial meaning in it, (c) that this world is, in the final analysis, an illusion, and (d) that the best course for man is to arrive, as soon as possible, at a state of *vairagya,* a turning away from the world, and to renounce the world and its activities in order to seek a Transcendental Reality or Existence which is in its nature or essence *entirely* different from the qualities and categories of the world of our ordinary experience.

It has, therefore, been held that Indian culture has been negative and pessimistic.

But as we read the Veda, which has been held as the source of the inspiration of the Indian culture, we find that it presents a dynamic interpretation of the world and assigns to action in the world a profound meaning and significance. It enjoins upon man to act rather than to renounce his activities. It places before man a method of action which has been discovered after a long and intense search by the Vedic seers. This method of action recognizes a secret relationship between the manifest and occult energies and actions that lie behind all that we physically see and experience. This relationship, it is held, is that of an interchange and, which is characteristically described as *yajna,* sacrifice. The Veda holds that the entire world is, in fact, a massive Energy flowing according to rhythm, which is that of an interchange between force and force, will and will, action and action. The Veda seizes upon this fundamental fact and points out that if man consciously follows the law of interchange and pursues it to its highest end, man will discover a state of being and power of action that remains always stable and integrated even though multiply varied and dynamic. This is the truth underlying the Vedic concept of the fundamental relationship between the earthly life, the supra-terrestrial life and the Supreme Reality, the supreme *Purusha*.

In practical terms, the Veda prescribes that every action of man should be a sacrifice offered by him to higher and higher forces and beings, to the *devas* and ultimately to the Supreme Being itself.

The world is thus not conceived as an illusion, although it grants that there is in this world an ignorance through which illusions are created in the world, and as a result of which our own view of the world is illusory. But the world itself, the movement of the world itself is not, according to the Veda, an illusion. Action of man, therefore, is not an illusion; it has meaning, and significance. Man is, therefore, not to renounce action, but on the contrary, he is to intensify his action until all his actions become a constant sacrifice offered to the Supreme.

There is no doubt that it was this emphasis on action and this insistence on action to be performed as a sacrifice that have provided a dynamic potency to the Indian culture. The secret of action that was discovered in the Veda seems to have been preserved in the age of the Upanishads, although there seems to have grown also a powerful tendency in some quarters to place knowledge in opposition to action, and to regard the former as superior to the latter. Nonetheless, we find that the Upanishadic wisdom recognized the meaningfulness of action and its spiritual and material utility. 'Kurvanneva iha karmani jijivishet shatam samah', (one should aspire to live a hundred years while performing actions here itself) - that is what is declared by the Isha Upanishad, which is the most compact enunciation of the quintessence of the Upanishadic teaching. The same insistence on action is to be found in the Gita where Sri Krishna expounds his greatest gospel of Karma Yoga, the path of action that leads to the union of man with the dynamic Will of the Supreme. It is, in fact, in the Gita that we find a comprehensive and abundant exposition of the principle of sacrifice (not ritualistic sacrifice) and of the method of performing actions as a sacrifice to the Divine.

The richness and opulence of life that was developed and

organized on a huge scale and upto an exceptional degree of excellence could be explained only on the basis of the great aim that was put forward by the Vedic rishis who perceived the inevitable connection between the dynamism of life and the ultimate fulfillment of man. It is true that the Vedic goal of life was only a prevision and a luminous seed, and therefore, capable of diverse developments and even inadequate and distorting translations during the succeeding ages. Thus, the later description of the Veda as a Karma Kanda, the science of action, as opposed to Jnana Kanda, the science of Knowledge, is an example of a diminutive understanding of the real purport of the Veda. It is also true that Poorva Mimamsa, one of the six orthodox philosophies of India, which came to represent the Vedic tradition, and which even today underlies most of the ritualistic and ceremonial practices of the Hindu orthodoxy, was also a specialized development of the profound truths of the Veda. But it must be noted that the Indian culture developed its dynamic life on some inborn intuition which was injected very powerfully at the very source in the early Vedic times and this has enabled India to build not only an astounding and exceptional structure of religion, philosophy, literature, art, architecture, and sciences of various kinds and skills and technologies of innumerable varieties, but also huge and powerful edifices of empire and statecraft and commerce and industry and opulence and richness and enjoyment in minutest detail of life. To say, therefore, that India has been governed by pessimism and by illusionism contradicts the very spirit that permeates the astonishingly dynamic culture of India.

It is true, however, that illusionism did play a role. It is true that there was a trend of thought and attitude which tended to look upon the world as a field of suffering and ignorance, and, therefore, something that must be rejected in order to achieve some supreme and perfect reality or state. But this trend became fully explicit only at a later stage after the sixth century B.C. The gospel of inaction and pessimism did become a predominant influence, and it was this that was responsible for a great weakening of the dynamic impulse of the Indian people. Even today's weakness of India can largely be traced to that influence.

But it must be stressed that the pessimistic tendencies had always to fight against other contending philosophies which gave a predominant or even exclusive importance to action and dynamism of life. Rejection of the world as an illusion and as a lie was challenged by several great and powerful exponents of the Vedanta.

If we ask, however, as to how the negative and pessimistic tendencies could at all succeed to become predominant, we shall find that India has been a special field of the search of the meaning of life, and that in this search it has not hesitated to affirm and experiment with hypotheses or propositions which are negative even to the highest degree. If we study this question in the historical perspective, we find that the Veda recognizes that there are three terms of existence which need to be put in an order of right relationship. These three terms are the supra-cosmic, the supra-terrestrial and the cosmic-terrestrial. The supra-cosmic is the supreme ineffable, (that moves and moves not) which is at once Kshara and Akshara, the dynamic and the static, and which is the supreme Mystery. The Veda recognizes that the terrestrial life is dependent upon the supra-terrestrial, which again is dependent on the supra-cosmic. The Vedic rishis discovered the laws and secrets of how man, the terrestrial being, could build his life by connecting himself consciously his relationships with the supra-terrestrial and supra-cosmic existence. The Vedic seers saw that the human life cannot be founded firmly in perfect relationship with the supra-terrestrial and the supra-cosmic without developing to a high level of perfection of the human action and human faculties of thought, will, emotions. The Veda, therefore, emphasized the need for an all-around perfection of the human body and of the human mind as also of the innumerable human energies of impulsion and motion. The Veda discovered the means of this development and laiddown *a system of an ordered and gradual development* of the human instrument so as to secure a progressive balance and harmony of growth and enjoyment of the human personality. The Vedic system of education perceived the need to accept and assimilate *all* aspects of human life, and it perceived at the same time, the need for a *balanced growth,* as opposed to the extreme insistences of the development of one aspect or tendency at the expense of some other aspect or tendency.

The Veda spoke of the possibility of perfection and of the integral perfection, and it spoke of this perfection as the state of immortality, *amritam.* But there is an important question in regard to which we do not find a clear and unambiguous answer. This question is: Can the integral perfection and immortality be fully established and manifested in the terrestrial physical life or is it something that is attainable, finally, by shedding the physical life?

There are indications to show that the Vedic rishis had a vision and experience of the possibility of realizing perfection and immortality even in the terrestrial physical life. The Veda speaks of the forefathers who have, according to it, reached this goal. But when we try to fathom deeper in search of the secret of this terrestrial perfection, we find ourselves arrested and we feel that there is something missing, something that still remains to be discovered and realized. It seems that the Veda, which is a record of the lofty adventure, is not a closed book, leaving nothing for the posterity for a new and further research. There is still something which the Veda is still in search of and which still needs to be enquired into. As the Veda itself declares, 'The priests of the world climb thee like a ladder, O hundred - powered. As one ascends from peak to peak, there is made clear the much that has still to be done'.

(brahmanas tva shatakrata
ud vamsham iva yomire.

Yat sanoh sanum aruhad
bhuri aspasta kartvam)

It seems, therefore, that the central question of Indian Culture has been to ask as to how it is possible to realize integral perfection in the terrestrial life and in physical body itself. This question was, it seems, answered in the Veda in a seed form. It even seems that it was realized that this aim was very difficult to achieve, and that it could probably be realized only with a Supreme effort in the terrestrial physical life. Because of the difficulties of this supreme effort, there seems to have been a tendency to assign greater and greater importance to the supra-terrestrial achievements in preference to the terrestrial ones. And in due course, there seems to have crept a powerful tendency to assign a subordinate value to the terrestrial life and to look upon the supra-terrestrial achievement as of lasting importance. In course of this development, more and more attention came to be paid to the methods and means by which one could escape more and more rapidly and easily from the labors of the terrestrial life. Only those labors and works came to be recognized which were indispensable for building up perfection in supra-terrestrial life. It is not surprising that this course of development could at one stage end up in the discovery of a state of experience or of being that would enable the individual to achieve the quickest escape from the world and its works.

Indeed, the methods of certain systems of yoga professed to give us precisely these very means of the most rapid escape from the world into a state of Nirvana, or of the inactive Brahman. They propounded the view that the terrestrial life is a result of Ignorance and of Desire and that it is an unending cycle of action (Karma) propelled by desire. It is here that we find the emergence of an attitude and approach to life which are in conflict with those which were developed and nourished by the Vedic teaching. In practical terms, this conflict can be explained as the one between the balanced growth, on the one hand, and exclusive and specialized growth, on the other. Whereas the Vedic approach underlined the need of the balanced growth of personality and of culture, the negative teaching preached a rapid and exclusive path by which the individual and the race could escape as rapidly as possible from the burdens and responsibilities of the terrestrial physical life.

If we are to understand Indian culture properly, we need to underline this conflict. It may be said that the foundations of Indian culture were laid by the Vedic approach. This approach required that the individual and social life of man should be so organized that the physical, vital and mental powers are helped to grow towards their perfection by means of a graded process which would provide to each stage of development the requisite station and stability as also the necessary drive for progress to higher and higher stations of activity and growth. This process was, according to the Veda, put in harmony with the requirements necessitated by the fact that our natural physical, vital and mental capacities and faculties are inter-twined with the powers and capacities and beings of the supra-terrestrial planes, and these again with the supra-cosmic reality. Thus the Indian culture based upon the Vedic ideal has a very wide and comprehensive basis, and it has a number of ladders of advancement, with varied programmes of integration of powers and capacities joining the terrestrial, the supra-terrestrial and the supra-cosmic into one vast and complex whole. This Vedic culture flourished not only for centuries but for millennia, and some of the high points of achievement of this culture are to be found in the ancient literature of India, particularly that of epics *(Ramayana and Mahabharata)*. But since the 6th century. B.C., there was introduced a current of culture which created confusion and a disbalancement in the vast organization of the balanced growth rooted in the teachings of the Veda. According to this disbalancing current, there is no need for balanced and graded development and for a vast and harmonious growth of the varied powers of the physical, vital and mental capacities and faculties. What was necessary was that each individual should be enabled as rapidly as possible to understand that the terrestrial labor of man was fundamentally meaningless and that he should develop only those capacities and powers which enable him to come out as soon as possible from the entire terrestrial life so as to enter into a supra-cosmic or acosmic Nirvana or Immobility.

With the introduction of this new current, Indian culture has suffered and there has come about in India a confusion of the ideals and progressive incompetence in dealing with the practical needs of human life.

It is not easy to suggest a solution by which the confused tangle of multi-dimensional Indian culture can be resolved. It has sometimes been suggested that India should go back to the Veda and to the Vedic ideal. On the other hand, the conditions of modern life are quite complex. There have entered into Indian life during the last one millennium certain motives of life which demand their own fulfillment or at least their right place in the totality of the cultural life of this vast sub-continent. Moreover, there has been an immense development of science and technology all over the world, and there is not only a rising tide of materialism but an effective invasion of materialistic culture. All this requires a new knowledge and a new power that could put all the elements of human culture, all the possible perfections of man on the earth into a new order of harmony and integration. As we saw earlier, the Vedic ideal itself was a luminous seed, but there intervened some deficiency which ultimately permitted the growth of negativism and pessimism. Thus, even while emphasizing the immense value of the Vedic ideal, and even while stressing the need to assimilate in the present hour the vast richness of the great Vedic culture, with all its positive results that have developed through the ages, we must underline the need to go forward and to hew a *new* path which would provide us the key to the perfectibility of the terrestrial and physical life.

Not only in India, but all over the world, there has been a dichotomy and opposition between the spiritual life and physical life. There has been the rejection of Matter by those who uphold the ideal of spiritual life, and there has been the rejection of the Spirit by those who uphold the ideal of a perfect physical life. It seems now as though these rejections have brought us through their consequences to a point in Thought and in Life where we are necessitated to look afresh and to question the facile proposition that Spirit and Matter are irreconcilable realities. We need to ask the question: What is Matter? We need to ask: What is Spirit? It is possible that the reality is neither the one nor the other, but something in which both are truly one.

Very likely we shall make a surprising discovery enabling us a new invention by which man in the world can be refashioned in a way that has so far not yet been conceived, or even if conceived to some extent, not conceived fully or realized.

In the direction of some such search seems to lie the path of the further progress of the Indian culture. This is the direction that has been explored in our own times by Sri Aurobindo, and this exploration gives us an assurance that Indian culture will provide a new guidance to the entire human race.

7

The Teacher and the Pupil

Ancient India conceived an intimate relationship between education and life. It looked upon education as a preparation for life and considered life a process of continuing education. It studied life in all its aspects and attempted to apply psychological principles and truths of life to education. One important consequence was to fix for education certain life-long objectives that require life-long effort to achieve and realize. These objectives were summarized in a triple formula which gave a wide and lofty framework to the ancient system of education.

Lead me from falsehood to truth.

Lead me from darkness to light.

Lead me from death to immortality.

असतो मा सद्गमय।

तमसो मा ज्योतिर्गमय।

मृत्योर्माऽमृतं गमय॥

This formula proved to be so potent that it governed the Indian system of education for ages. Even today, remote as we are from that ancient ethos, we refer to it constantly for fresh inspiration.

To the ancient thinkers and sages, the ideals of truth, light and immortality constituted a triune unity, each subsisting in the other. Truth meant to them not an isolated fact, but one vast unity of the Objective Fact in which the multiplicity of facts and phenomena finds its essential oneness. Light meant to them a state of plenary consciousness in which essence and multiplicity is comprehended in a vast, undivided, unified and integral concentration. That state of consciousness in which the reality of unity and oneness is comprehended was found by them to be an imperturbable and imperishable state of immortality, a state in which one can permanently dwell and through which one can effectuate extraordinary transmutations of the process of the mind, life and body.

That Objective Fact, self-luminous and imperishable, which comprehends multiplicity in oneness, was named variously in the early records of Indian knowledge. The Veda, the earliest record, described it as the 'One Existent which the Wise call by various names' *(ekam sad, vipra bahudha vadanti)*.* The Upanishads, the later records, describe it sometimes as sat, the Pure Existent, and sometimes as asat, the Non-Existent or the ineffable that transcends any particular description. The Upanishads also describe it as the Unknowable, an indefinable 'x', the Brahman, That (tat), the other which can be seized only by a process that dismisses every description by pronouncing 'not that, not that' (neti neti). The largest positive description the Upanishads gives of that 'x', that Something Else, is Sachchidananda (the conscious and delightful Existent).

The Upanishads admit clearly and unambiguously that the knowledge of the Sat or the Brahman is neither intellectual nor anti-intellectual. Indeed, it is beyond the grasp of the senses, *atindriyam* but it is still *buddhigrahyam*,** seizable by the intellect. Pure Reason, it may be said, has the idea of essence, and by developing this idea, can arrive at some concept of the Brahman, even though Brahman is more than essence. However, according to strict criteria, knowledge is determined both through idea and through direct, abiding and undeniable experience. The strength of the Vedic and Upanishadic assertions is that they were arrived at by centuries of experiment in discovering and practising certain profound methods by which the Objective Fact, the Substance, that Multiple One, the simple-complex, the mysterious 'x' the Sat or the Brahman can be seized and known in direct experience.

It is said that existence is what we knock into; it is something we cannot think away, it stands and cannot be obliterated. But in normal experience, our subjective apparatus imposes its own categories on the object of experience, and we are thus prevented from experiencing the truly existent object—if, indeed, there is such a thing. We experience, to use Kant's terminology, quantity, quality, relation and modality, in addition to two forms of intuition, Space and Time. But we fail to experience the Object-in-itself, the

**Rig Veda*, Mandala I, Sukta 164, Verse 46.
***Gita*, VI, 21.

Existence-in-itself. The question is whether we can remove the blinders of our subjective mental consciousness, look freely at truth, and experience in a state of total objectivity the reality as it is.

The ancient Indian educational theory affirms that it is possible to transcend the limitations of sense-bound experience and reason-bound consciousness, and that the most fundamental object of education is to prepare the pupil to free himself from those limitations and attain that level of knowledge where he can dwell permanently in existent reality, in light and in immortality.

The early Indian educators made a distinction between Vidya and Avidya, between the knowledge of Existence-in-itself, in its totality and multiple manifestation, and the knowledge of multiplicity alone, without the comprehension of the underlying unity. And it was laid down that the aim of education, of life-long education, was to lead the individual to the knowledge which liberates from the limitations of Avidya, *Sa Vidya ya vimuktaye.*

If we study the Veda and the Upanishads in a truly scientific spirit, unprejudiced by any *a priori* dogma that the human limitations of consciousness cannot be transcended, we shall find that the authors of these ancient records were themselves true scientists and experimenters. Those thinkers and seers devoted all their energies to the study of human psychology so as to discover the methods by which we can attain freedom from our ordinary limitations. This discovery was the most significant achievement of ancient India. As Sri Aurobindo pointed out, '. . . the seers of ancient India had, in their experiments and efforts at spiritual training and the conquest of the body, perfected a discovery which in its importance to the future of human knowledge dwarfs the divinations of Newton and Galileo, even the discovery of the inductive and experimental method in Science was not more momentous...'[*]

This discovery was the discovery of Yoga. The ancient seers made a distinction between religion and Yoga. Religion is a matter of belief, rituals and ceremonies, even though it may involve an inner practice of moral and spiritual discipline. Yoga, on the other hand, focuses on psychology and on developing the psychological faculties and powers by which the highest Object of Knowledge can be experienced. To the Yogin, what matters is that direct

[*]Sri Aurobindo, The Upanishads, Sri Aurobindo Birth Centenary Library, vol.12, p.6.

experience, attained by psychological enlargement, psychological purification and psychological revolution. Just as physical science starts with the natural phenomenon of lightning and utilizes various means to generate, control and distribute electricity on an increasing scale, even so Yoga takes up the ordinary psychological functioning of body, life and mind and discovers methods by which these psychological functionings can be brought to their highest pitch and then generated, controlled and used at will for the objects in view.

There were, indeed, specializations. Hatha Yoga, for example, concentrated on the subtle workings of the body, and by means of controlling and purifying these workings achieved astonishing results, not only of physical health and vigor but even of preparing the individual for deeper spiritual realizations. Raja Yoga specialized in dealing with mental vibrations and discovered methods by which the stuff of consciousness can be controlled and brought to a state of complete stillness in which the Object of Knowledge stands out clearly and luminously. The Yoga of Knowledge, the Yoga of Divine Love and the Yoga of Action took up, respectively, the workings of cognition, affection and conation, and arrived at extraordinary experiences of higher levels of consciousness and their corresponding objects of knowledge.

Those ancient seers also made a distinction between Yoga and philosophy. Philosophy was restricted to mean intellectual reasoning about the ultimate source of things or intellectual transcription of spiritual experience. It was recognized that Yoga transcended intellectual methods of thought and attempted to revolutionize the ego-bound operations of thinking, feeling and action so as to arrive at a new and heightened functioning of the higher self, the Atman or the Brahman.*

In spite of its specialized domains and crowning realizations, yogic research constantly strove to combine various systems of

*In the Brihadaranyaka Upanishad, it is said: 'Therefore let the seeker, after he has done with learning, wish to stand by real strength (knowledge of the Self) which enables us to dispense with all other knowledge' (iii,5,I). In the same Upanishad, it is said again, 'He should not seek after the knowledge of the books, for that is mere weariness of the tongue' (iv,4,21). Describing the higher Self, the Taittiriya Upanishad says: 'Before whom words and thought recoil, not finding him' (ii,4). The Katha Upanishad declares: 'Not by teaching is the Atman attained, nor by intellect, nor by much knowledge of books' (i,2,23).

Yoga for purposes of arriving at synthetic and composite results. The Veda itself represented a certain kind of synthesis. Upanishadic seers made further research, recovered the Vedic Yoga, and brought about a fresh synthesis. Yoga, like science, was never looked upon as a closed book; like science, Yoga encouraged fresh quest and fresh realizations. Yoga came thus to be recognized as a science *par excellence.*

We have in the records of the Vedas and the Upanishads the names of those who developed this great science of yoga. The generic name is Rishi, the illumined seer, standing above the world and yet uplifting it by his upward gaze, unruffled concentration and compassionate wisdom. It was the Rishi who came to be acknowledged as the teacher and revered as Guru or Acharya. It is to the Rishi that the pupils went in search of training and knowledge, and the ancient Indian teacher-pupil relationship came to be determined by the profound and even inscrutable ways by which the teachers and pupils, Gurus and Shishyas, developed their modes and methods of exploring knowledge, discovering the aim and meaning of life, and practicing disciplines for arriving at psychological perfection.

The names of the Vedic Rishis still reverberate in the Indian atmosphere, inspiring veneration and obeisance—the names of Vishwamitra and Vashishtha, Vamadeva and Bharadwaja, Madhuchhandas and Dirghataṃas, Gritsamada and Medhatithi. Some of the prose Upanishads have a vivid narrative which restores for us, though only in brief glimpses, the picture of that extraordinary stir and movement of enquiry and passion for the highest knowledge which made the Upanishads possible.

We see here how the soul of India was born, and we come to recognize the Vedas and Upanishads as not only the fountainhead of Indian philosophy and spirituality, of Indian art, poetry and

[*]These great names are those to whom various parts of the Rig Veda are attributed. The Rig Veda, as we possess it, is arranged in ten books. They are called Mandalas. Six of the Mandalas are attributed each to the hymns of a single Rishi or a family of Rishis. Thus the second Mandala is devoted chiefly to the Suktas of the Rishi Gritsamada, the third Mandala and the Seventh Mandala to Vishwamitra and Vashishtha, respectively, the fourth to Vamadeva, the sixth to Bharadwaja. The Fifth is occupied by the hymns of the house of Atri. Other Mandalas contain the hymns of several Rishis and Rishikas. The prominent names of Rishikas in the Rig Veda are: Romasha, Lopamudra, Apala, Kadru, Vishwavara.

literature, but also of Indian education and of the Indian tradition of teacher-pupil relationship.

The most important idea governing the ancient system of education was that of perfection, for developing the mind and soul of man. Indian education aimed at helping the individual to grow in the power and force of certain large universal qualities which in their harmony build a higher type of manhood. In Indian thought and life, this was the ideal of the best, the law of the good or noble man, the discipline laid down for the self-perfecting individual. This ideal was not a purely moral or ethical conception, although that element pre-dominated; it was also intellectual, social, aesthetic, the flowering of the whole ideal man, the perfection of the total human nature. We meet in the Indian conception of best, shreshtha, the most varied qualities. In the heart benevolence, beneficence, love, compassion, altruism, long-suffering, liberality, kindliness, patience; in the character courage, heroism, energy, loyalty, continence, truth, honour, justice, faith, obedience and reverence where these were due, but power too to govern and direct, a fine modesty and yet a strong independence and noble pride; in the mind wisdom and intelligence and love of learning, knowledge of all the best thought, openness to poetry, art and beauty, an educated capacity and skill in works; in the inner being piety, love of God, seeking after the highest, the spiritual turn; in social relations and conduct a strict observance of all social obligations as father, son, husband, brother, kinsman, friend, ruler or subject, master or servant, prince or warrior or worker, king or sage. This ideal is clearly portrayed in the written records of ancient India. It was the creation of an ideal and rational mind, both spirit-wise and worldly-wise, deeply spiritual, nobly ethical, firmly yet flexibly intellectual, scientific and aesthetic, patient and tolerant of life's difficulties and human weakness, but arduous in self-discipline.

The ancient Indian system of education developed as a part of the general system of Indian culture. This system at once indulged and controlled man's nature; it fitted him for his social role; it stamped on his mind the generous ideal of an accomplished humanity, refined, harmonious in all its capacities, ennobled in all its members; but it placed before him too the theory and practice of Yoga, the theory and practice of a higher change, familiarized him with the concept of a spiritual existence and sowed in him a hunger for the divine and the infinite. The pupil was not allowed to forget that he had within him a higher self beyond his little personal ego, and that numerous ways and disciplines were provided by which he could realize this higher self or at least turn and follow at a distance this higher aim according to his capacity and nature, adhikara. Around him he saw and revered the powerful teachers who practised and were mighty masters of these disciplines.

In the Indian system of education, there was a great deal of emphasis on discipline. The life of the pupil began with a resolve to impose upon himself the ideal and practice of Brahmacharya, which meant not only physical continence, but a constant burning aspiration for the knowledge of the Brahman. This one ideal uplifted the physical, vital and mental energies in unified concentration to achieve self-knowledge and self-mastery. For this reason, the pupil came to be called the Brahmacharin, one who has resolved to follow the discipline of Brahmacharya. *Vratam charishyami*—I shall resolutely follow my vow, is what the pupil resolves when he embarks upon his journey of discipleship.

Pursuit of truth was a part of the discipline of Brahmacharya; so also was the pursuit of kindliness, harmony and love, *ahimsa*. Practice of renunciation of the sense of personal possession of things and relations, renunciation of covetousness that leads to theft and collection of personal possessions, were also part of a pupil's self-discipline. In addition, the pupil was expected to develop purity—purity of the body, purity of emotions and purity of thought.

Swadhyaya (self-study) was the corner-stone of the pupil's discipline and method of learning. The pupil was expected to develop extraordinary powers of memory, imagination and thought. The predominance of oral tradition necessitated the cultivation of the power of memory; the high content of philosophical and spiritual knowledge necessitated the cultivation of subtlety and complexity of thought; the natural setting of the Ashrams and Gurukulas in the open forest, where nature could be an intimate friend and companion, necessitated the cultivation of the power of inner communion, imagination and natural delight.

That the life of the pupil was vigorous and rigorous cannot be doubted. But it must not be supposed that there was any absence of mirth and joy. In some of the accounts of life in the Ashrams there is ample evidence to show that the system of education was flexible, free from the rigidities found in the lecture and examination-oriented system in which our present system of education is imprisoned. A good deal of individual attention was paid to every pupil. The teacher was not expected to demand from the pupil more than the highest effort of which he was capable. The teacher varied his method with each pupil, and education was devised to suit each individual's need of growth and development. In *Abhijnana Shakuntalam*, Kalidasa gives a beautiful portrayal of the Ashram of Kanva, a great Rishi revered by common people and kings alike. In this Ashram there were both boys and girls, and while the atmosphere was surcharged with tapasya, self-discipline, there was also fun and frolic among friends. No feeling of rigidity is portrayed in this beautiful drama. There is, rather, restrained charm, joy and beauty. Other accounts, too, such as those in the Ramayana and the Mahabharata, describe the color and warmth of the interplay of the forces of human nature, and give examples of how the teacher dealt with this interplay with gentle firmness guided by mature experience and wisdom.*

The teacher, the Rishi, was the seer who had lived the fullness of life and had often led the life of a householder. In some accounts the Rishi's wife was also a Rishi in her own right and lived in the Ashram along with her husband, providing material care for the pupils. The Ashram was veritable Gurukula, where the pupils were loved and cared for as members of the Guru's family.

In those times the task of the teacher was to awaken more than to instruct. It was understood that true knowledge depended on the cultivation of powers of concentration, which in turn depended

*In the Mahabharata (i.70), there is a description of Kanva's hermitage. It was situated on the banks of the Malini, a tributary of the Sarayu River. Numerous hermitages stretched round the central hermitage. At this Ashram, there were specialists in each of the four Vedas; in Phonetics, Metrics, Grammar, and Nirukta. There were also philosophers well-versed in the science of the Absolute. There were logicians. There were also specialists in the physical sciences and arts. In this forest university, the study of every available branch of learning was cultivated. In the Ramayana (vi,126; ii, 90-2), we have an interesting description of the hermitage of Rishi Bharadwaja at Prayaga. This hermitage was one of the biggest of the times. The Ashram was equipped with stalls to accommodate the royal elephants and horses; there were mansions and palaces and gateways. A separate royal guest house was furnished with beds, seats, vehicles, coverlets and carpets, stores of food. The Ashram also entertained its royal guests with performances by musicians and dancing girls.

upon great quietude of the mind and absence of demands of impatient and hurried work. It was also acknowledged that some of the greatest truths needed to be practised by voluntary choice and persistent, dedicated discipline. The system of education provided ample opportunities for the pupil to experience the significance of free choice, particularly the choice between the good and the pleasant, *shréyas* and *préyas*. What was discouraged was personal indulgence or undisciplined preference; but the very object of education implied free choice at every important stage of a pupil's growth. In other words, freedom of choice and an increasing experience of spiritual freedom blended together in that system of education.

It is sometimes argued that the ancient Indian tradition gave too much importance to reverence to the teacher.* It is contended that the teacher was unduly placed on the highest pedestal and that this developed authoritarianism in the teacher and slavishness in the pupil. How shall we meet this criticism? What truth lies behind it? In the course of history, when the Rishi came to be replaced by the Pandit, the illumined seer by the erudite scholar, there was quite often a tendency on the part of the Pandit to arrogate to himself the natural power, authority and influence of the Rishi, and this did injure the tradition. Further degeneration came about when the pandit was replaced by ordinary sophists, debaters and bookish teachers. At the same time, it must be said that the good Pandits and ordinary teachers refrained from arrogating to themselves the authority of the Rishi. Indeed, the ideal we find in the ancient Indian system is that it is not only by obediently serving the teacher but also by repeated and full questioning that the pupil can gain the right knowledge, *pari prashnena, pari sevaya*.

Actually, reverence for the teacher was enjoined upon the pupil for three main reasons. In the first place, Indian culture and consequently the Indian system of education strove to subordinate the demands of the ego to the demands of society, of the world and of the higher self. An attempt was made to create systems and practices—through rule, tradition or other means—by which the demands of the higher self were given a predominant position. In

*One well-known verse speaks of Guru as Brahma, as Vishnu and as Maheshwara. He is equated with the Supreme Absolute Being.

गुरुर्ब्रह्मा गुरुर्विष्णु: गुरुर्देवो महेश्वरः।
गुरुः साक्षात् परब्रह्म तस्मै श्री गुरवे नमः॥

fact, not only the teacher, but the mother and the father and even the guest were given a place of high reverence. As the Taittiriya Upanishad says: *Matri devo bhava, pitri devo bhava, acharya devo bhava, atithi devo bhava.* ('Let thy father be unto thee as thy God, and thy mother as thy Goddess whom thou adorest. Serve the master as a God, and as a God the stranger within thy dwelling.')

The second reason was that the Rishi represented not only a mature worldly and scholarly wisdom but also a high spiritual realization, and thus was to be doubly revered. In modern days, where knowledge is easily available through books and other means of communication, our full appreciation of knowledge is likely to be considerably diminished. Thus we may not be able to understand why the Guru was assigned high and exceptional reverence. But we must note that the Vedic and Upanishadic periods were marked by an intense quest for new knowledge. There was, as it were, an unquenchable thirst, and only the thirsty know what gratitude is due to the one who quenches the thirst. In that context, then, reverence for the teacher was not something imposed upon the pupil; the real seeker became psychologically impelled to revere anyone who had knowledge and could transmit it effectively to him. This was particularly true when the knowledge sought after was not only pragmatic and intellectual but spiritual. For among all human endeavours, spiritual endeavour is the most difficult, beset with the greatest difficulties. In certain circumstances, the pursuit of spiritual knowledge requires vigilant direction and guidance. Spiritual search is like a search in a virgin forest, and the law of that search exacts from the seeker the highest price of self-sacrifice and consecration. The guide and teacher on the spiritual path, therefore, deserves the highest reverence. The intricacies and hazards of the spiritual endeavour are known to the teacher, and it is often unwise to reveal them to the seeker in advance. Spiritual discoveries and realizations imply major psychological surgery. These operations the pupil cannot perform by himself; a teacher is needed. And just as a doctor demands from the patient a high degree of trust and obedience, so does the teacher of the spiritual path.

But there is a third reason for the reverence demanded of the pupil for the teacher. The Indian educational and yogic system recognized that the real teacher is the supreme Brahman seated within oneself, and sooner rather than later, the seeker must discover the inner teacher and the inner guide.

The necessity for the pupil to have the external word or the external guidance of a teacher is then seen to be a concession to human limitations. We require external aids until we realize the true inner Aid. This being the case, the external teacher comes to represent to the seeker the Supreme Brahman. Therefore, the reverence due to the Supreme is offered by the seeker to the external teacher. On his part, the external teacher, if he knows his true position, looks upon his task as a trust given to him from above. He realizes the relativity of his importance. Knowing that the real teacher is seated within the pupil, he hands over the task of guidance to that inner guide as soon as possible. Until then, he devotes all his energies to one single aim, the flowering of the pupil's faculties and the awakening of the inner guide seated within the pupil's heart. It is to such a teacher that the ancient tradition of India assigned highest reverence.

The good teacher is not content with his own self-knowledge. He constantly seeks fresh knowledge and attempts to share it with other seekers. His prayer is that of the Rishi in the Taittiriya Upanishad, who says:

May the Brahmacharins come unto me. Swaha!
From here and there may the Brahmacharins come unto me. Swaha!
May the Brahmacharins set forth unto me. Swaha!
May the Brahmacharins attain to peace of soul. Swaha!*

आ मा यन्तु ब्रह्मचारिणः स्वाहा।
वि मा यन्तु ब्रह्मचारिणः स्वाहा।
प्र मा यन्तु ब्रह्मचारिणः स्वाहा।
दमायन्तु ब्रह्मचारिणः स्वाहा।
शमायन्तु ब्रह्मचारिणः स्वाहा।

The good teacher as conceived in the ancient system of India interweaves his own life with the life of his pupils. He aspires and prays not for himself alone but also for his pupils. Togetherness is the watchword of the good teacher.

He prays:

Together may He protect us,
Together may He possess us,
Together may we make unto us strength and virility;

*Taittiriya Upanishad, Shikshavalli, chapter 4.

May our study be full to us of light and power.
May we never hate.*

And what is the advice that the good teacher gives to his pupils? He says, 'Speak truth, walk in the way of thy duty, neglect not the study of knowledge. Thou shalt not be negligent of truth; thou shalt not be negligent of thy duty, thou shalt not be negligent of welfare; thou shalt not be negligent towards thy increase and thy thriving; thou shalt not be negligent of the study and teaching of the highest Truth'.

During the Vedic and Upanishadic periods, and even later, there was an emphasis on the pursuit of an integral aim of life, which determined the discipline of integral education. Both the material and spiritual poles of being had their place in this system. The ancient Sanskrit adage, *shareeram adyam khalu dharma sadhanam* (a sound body is the veritable instrument of the pursuit of the ideal law of life) underlined the importance of physical education. There was also a clear recognition that the fullness of physical, vital and mental culture was necessary for arriving at spiritual perfection. And if we study the Yoga of the Veda in its inmost significance, we find that there was an intense research into the possibilities of spiritual manifestation in physical life. There was a secret knowledge that the highest light is contained in the darkest caves of the physical or the inconscient, and that one must descend into the depths of darkness to recover that highest light. In practical terms, this implied not rejection of physical and material life but an intensive cultivation and transformation of that life.

It is true that there was a gradual deviation from the original Vedic conception of life and education. Much of it was recovered by the seers of the Upanishads, and the integrality of spirit and matter was preserved in some of their teachings. But already a kind of exclusivism had become manifest during the Upanishadic Age. Later, sharp distinctions came to be made between Spirit and Matter, and a denunciation of material life became more and more predominant. The call of the spirit and a recoil from matter characterize powerful movements of Indian thought. This affected the educational system, and the original impulse of integral education was lost. The consequences have been disastrous, and today we are in a deep crisis.

*Taittiriya Upanishad, Brahmanandavalli, chapter I.

But is it a question merely of recovering that original impulse? Are we to propose revivalism? This is a matter of controversy. Although what was valuable in the ancient system should be preserved and developed, if we examine the spirit of the Indian Renaissance and the task it has set out to accomplish, we find that a mere revival of the old will not suffice; we shall have to admit new elements and new attitudes which are valuable for preparing the future humanity.

The Indian Renaissance strove for an India that is genuinely Indian and genuinely universal. India became free not only for itself but for the sake of humanity. Free India has to take up the deeper problems that today confront humanity as a whole. As Sri Aurobindo points out:

> Mankind is passing today through an evolutionary crisis in which is contained the choice of its destiny.

It is in that context that Sri Aurobindo undertook a program of research involving the discovery of new knowledge in the light of which a new synthesis relevant to the needs of today and tomorrow can be created. The secret of that synthesis, as pointed out by Sri Aurobindo, is the manifestation of Spirit in Matter, leading to an unprecedented perfection and even a mutation of the human species. Sri Aurobindo's discovery of the Supermind and its possibility of full operation in physical life may be regarded as the most significant gift of renascent India to humanity's effort to overcome its crisis.

This has also a momentous consequence for education. The new education that must be built should be a new kind of integral education that will aim at organizing that discovery in more and more concrete forms. This is a matter of continuing experimentation and research.*

*In Appendix I some passages are presented from the Veda and the Upanishads which will provide a few glimpses of the aspirations and realisations of the Rishis, who were teachers, and of the early system of Indian concept of education.

8

The Rishi and the Society

It is difficult to assess the immensity of the influence that the Vedic rishis exercised over the people in the midst of whom they lived and with whom they had direct or indirect contact. But there is no doubt that the Vedic rishis were held in highest esteem by people of all categories and that their advice was sought and implemented so readily that they were able to cast the early forms of social life in some flexible mould so as to secure progressive unfoldment and development of culture on some sound and original lines over the centuries and millennia.

Three important points may, in this regard, be noted.

I. In the first place, the image and ideal of rishihood was so strongly impressed upon the society that the rishi has been held throughout the ages as the object of the highest reverence. The word of the rishi, whether of the past or of the present, has had always an authority greater than that of any other leader of the society. Even the law of the state was very often obeyed and accepted by the people only when it received sanction from the rishi. Often, the word of the rishi had an automatic authority of the law of the state. Many rapid changes in society were effected in certain important periods of Indian history, not by any struggle of the people or by any legislative process, but simply by what the rishi said or advised.

II. There was an explicit recognition in the society of a distinction between the rishi and the priest. The mark of the rishi is that he has lived in fullness the human life and *experienced* the true truth of man and the universe. He lives in the truth and hears the truth and reveals the truth and the limitations of time and space do not apply to him. At the highest, the rishi has the knowledge of the past, of the present and the future, possessed of *trikalajnana* and *trikaladrishti* (the knowledge of the three times, past, present and future, and the perception of the three times). The rishi has not only the knowledge but he has also the wisdom. The rishi is not only a man of contemplation but also a warrior, a hero, capable of handling the most difficult situations of human life and giving an unambiguous and sure guidance. The rishi is not a mere transmitter of tradition, but he can, if necessary, break the tradition and establish the new. The rishi was not merely a scholar, often he was not a scholar at all, but he could command knowledge whenever needed. He was not a mental being, but one who had transcended the limitations of the mental consciousness and had a direct access to superior modes of knowledge and action. All this was recognized by masses of people throughout the Indian history, and it is a significant fact that throughout the ages India has thrown up a long and unbroken line of rishis of various orders (even among the rishis there are recognized gradations), and there is hardly a period in which there have not been at least a few rishis recognized and revered by the people.

III. The rishi alone was and has been recognized as the real teacher, the guru. He alone has the authority and power to mediate between the seeker and the supreme Object of seeking. He has the power of evocation, and he can, if he so chooses and feels necessary to break the seals of the seeker's consciousness, lead him to the direct experience of the reality. He has the right word of instruction and the right mantra of initiation. He is himself an example of the ideal that he places before the seeker, and he has a spontaneous power of influence, not indeed of any external authority or arrogant arbitrariness, but that which flows from his inmost being to the inmost being of the seeker. He is, in fact, a teacher because he does not teach, he is simply a channel of the real Teacher who is seated in the heart of every living and thinking being. He is a brother of brothers, a child leading the children.

Such has been the concept of the rishi as the teacher in Indian culture. And those who practised teaching but did not reach the stage of rishihood were not accorded the highest reverence that is due to the guru. They were *acharyas*, but not rishis. The *acharyas* were respected for their learning, for their proficiency, for their special standing in their respective disciplines of knowledge and art, but they received the highest reverence only when they rose to rishihood. The rishi was the ideal even for the *acharyas*, and every teacher has been enjoined in Indian culture to grow progressively into the image of the rishi.

A remarkable feature of the institution of the rishi is the special place accorded to the rishis by the rulers, politicians, statesmen and administrators. Rishi was to them not merely a spiritual preceptor but also an adviser in regard to state policy and state affairs. The rishi was approached by them for counsel and his counsel was accepted. And this determined the major developments of the political and social activities and institutions. Often rishis presided over the special sacrifices as *Rajsuya* and *Ashavmedha*. And there are traditions of rishis acting as permanent political advisers. In fact, there arose in India an arrangement whereby rishis became as a rule principal advisers or ministers, and they exercised supervening influence in kings' councils.

It was from this arrangement that, as varna system became more and more pronounced, there grew a tradition of Kshatriya king and a Brahmin minister. The Kshatriyas represented the qualities not only of courage, heroism, but also of power and strength, and ambition and desire for rule. The Kshatriyas represented, predominantly, the principle of vital force, and it was known in Indian psychology that the vital force, if left unbridled or untransformed, could easily become a source of mis-adventure and even of destruction. Happily, the Brahmin as a minister provided to the Kshatriya king the right guidance and inspiration which the pure intelligence of intellect and intuition can give. For the Brahmins, even when far below the Rishis in their attainments, represented the qualities of the clarity of the intellect and wise intuitive perception as also wide knowledge of sciences and arts and of affairs and men. The Brahmin often lacked the drive and intuition and force of action, and thus he needed as his complement the Kshatriya, just as the Kshatriya needed the Brahmin as his complement. This combination of the Brahmin and Kshatriya in regard to political power and activity constituted a wise and powerful element in Indian culture, and this was certainly one of the important factors in the stability and ordered progress of many kingdoms and states that flourished from age to age. This system was not without its defects, and there were often rivalries between the king and the minister for supremacy. But, on the whole, these rivalries were a part of the natural friction among powerful personalities. In due course, however, the tradition began to break and after the first millennium of the Christian era, this system operated only in some parts and only for short periods from time to time. New systems of political organization were introduced, and after centuries, under the British rule, an alien way of rule and administration prevailed over most parts of India.

It is, however, important to note that the basic Vedic idea of the rishi as the seer and knower and as a guide of the individual and collective life has remained alive, at least to a certain degree, even in the present-day India. And there is even today an imagination and conviction in some deep recesses of Indian thought and feeling that there cannot be right and wise and ideal governance of society unless the rishi or a group of rishis guide and exercise political power. In some such conviction, Indian culture is today seeking, mostly secretly, to bring to the surface the wisdom and guidance of the rishis.

9

The Veda, Intuition and Philosophy

The influence of the Veda is remarkably perceptible in the development and growth of Indian science, art, literature and philosophy. It has been affirmed that the Veda contains a vast body of scientific knowledge and that it anticipates even the most modern ideas of Physics, Chemistry and Astronomy. It is true that it is difficult to prove this affirmation since such a proof would require a vast and difficult research. But there is no doubt that among many possible interpretations of the Veda there could be a possible line which could open up various clues and deliver to us some startling conclusions which would prove that the Vedic seers had by some special methods of knowledge known what the modern science has now discovered or is still groping to discover. In any case, it is true that the Indian scientists who developed astonishing ideas and concepts of Mathematics, Astronomy, Medicine and Physics and Chemistry refer to the Veda and Vedantic knowledge as the source of their inspiration and knowledge.

In regard to philosophy, Veda occupies a very special position. The Indian system of philosophy that specializes in logic and epistemology (Nyaya Philosophy) distinguishes between various means of knowledge, and affirms that the Veda itself is the supreme means of knowledge. And this is the position which is accepted by all the other philosophies which claim to have been derived from the Veda. These philosophies include, apart from Nyaya, also Vaisheshika, Sankhya, Yoga, Poorva Mimamsa, Uttara Mimamsa and the varied interpretations of the philosophy of the Uttara Mimamsa, notably the philosophies of Shankara, Ramanuja, Madhwa, Nimbarka, Vallabha, Chaitanya and others.

The Veda is also known as Shruti. The word 'shruti' literally means that which is heard. Now it has been contended that the Vedic knowledge is a result of a special hearing. This hearing is not sensual, but it is something which occurs when all senses are withdrawn and when even thought process is silenced and surpassed. It is a phenomenon that occurs on a plane of consciousness known as that of Intutiion (a word which hardly connotes what it is intended to connote).

In other words, it has been held that intuition is a means of knowledge that is distinguishable very clearly from the knowledge derived by senses or by reasoning or by analogy. The knowledge derived by intuition is not only direct but it springs from the identity of the subject and the object which are related to each other in the process of knowledge. This process does not need to depend upon the exericse of the senses. This knowledge sees even when eyes are closed, it hears even when ears are sealed. Again, this knowledge is not ratiocinative. It does not strive to arrive at a conclusion on the basis of premises and by the help of some universal principles. This knowledge is immediate, there are no premises in this process. The conclusions are themselves the states of experience intimately identical with the objects of knowledge. Finally, this knowledge is not open to fallacies, doubts or errors, since these deficiencies belong only to senses or to the processes of reasoning. The intuitive knowledge is, therefore, regarded as authentic and true. Just as the light of the sun can be proved only through light itself, even so the light of this knowledge can be proved through this very light. This knowledge is, therefore, also known as *swayam prabha*, self-luminous.

It is affirmed that the entire gamut of the Vedic knowledge is intuitive. It is self-luminous and true.

On this basis, it has been held that the Vedic knowledge is authentic and authoritative. Also, when there are disputes arising from conflicts of sense-observation and of diverse philosophical reasonings, they can all be resolved by referring to the authentic knowledge of the Veda.

An important element of Indian philosophy which admits the Veda as an authority is that it does not accept the conclusions of philosophical reasoning as conclusive, unless they are supported also by the pronouncements of the Veda. Indian philosophy, therefore, considers Shruti as a conclusive criterion of truth. Thus we find Indian philosophers adducing philosophical arguments in support of their philosophical point of view, but their final argument is always a statement from the Veda. And it is this statement from the Veda which brings the debate to the final end.

It is necessary to distinguish between the authority that is assigned to the Veda in Indian philosophy from the authority that is assigned to dogma.

It is true that both of them claim unquestionablity and both of them claim superiority to reason. But while the authority of dogma cannot be verified in any fresh or repeatable experience, the authority of the Veda can, it is held, be verified in a fresh and repeatable experience, even in *an abiding* experience. Thus when it is said that Indian philosophy admits Shruti as the final authority, what is really meant is that Indian philosophy admits experience - intuitive experience - as the final authority.

This subject of the authority of the Veda in Indian philosophy is extremely important, and as a matter of a purely philosophical discussion, it is a highly controversial issue. Much of this controversy is due to the fact that in course of history, Veda did come to be used as an unquestionable dogma.

It is this tendency to reduce freshness of intuitive knowledge to a body of dogmatic revelations that produced a reaction among some of the robust minds and spirits in India. Thus there arose in India a very powerful anti-Vedic tradition, and there are a number of philosophies which refuse to accept the authority of the Veda. The important among them are the philosophies of Jainism, Buddhism, Charvaka.

It must be said, however, that the Vedic seers themselves did not regard their own experiences to be used dogmatically. The Vedas themselves are a record of experiences and they were never intended to be a dogmatic authority. The Upanishadic seers did not look upon the Veda as a dogma. They endeavoured to compare their experiences among those of the contemporaries and of the Vedic forefathers. Fortunately, this tradition of comparison and verification of the Vedantic knowledge did not die away completely. And thus it was possible in India to continue spiritual research and to arrive at *new* spiritual truths. And it seems that it is this tradition which has now begun to gain ascendancy and the future of Indian philosophy is sure to break a new ground that will affirm intuitive experience as an authority and superior means of knowledge but which will reject it as any binding dogma.

10

The Veda and the concept of Dharma

The Veda has been regarded as the foundation of Indian Culture and the Rishis of the Veda have been revered throughout the ages in India as having heard the truth and revealed it and thus given perennial wisdom to guide the development of the future.

One of the most dominant ideas of Indian culture has been that of Dharma, and this has been a consequence of the Vedic discovery of the *Rita*, the Right. According to the Vedic Rishis, there is, at the summit of consciousness, a power of action which arranges forces and activities of the universe by an automatic harmony of relationships, movements and results. The right law of this automatic harmony is the *Rita*. The Rita itself is founded in the truth of the Reality and of the universe, *(satyam)*, and its field of action is the totality which is the infinite vast (brihat). It is by the discovery of the Rita that, according to the Vedic Rishis, the human consciousness is delivered from the *crookedness* of the ignorant mental action. The actions of truth are direct and straight and the law of this directness and straightness is the Rita. There is no groping in the Truth-consciousness, and there is no attempt at inventing devices for initiating and accomplishing any action. Thus, when the Truth-consciousness is achieved, there is automaticity and spontaneity of action as also the right rhythm of action. Since the action of Truth-Consciousness is automatic and spontaneous, it cannot be fixed by any arbitrary rule of the mental intelligence or by any pragmatic or utilitarian necessities of individual or collective life. The Rita, therefore, cannot be prescribed or circumscribed by any legislation or any man-made law. Rita is, indeed, the right law of action, but it issues from the vast consciousness of the truth, and it is thus superior to any human standards of action or any laws of the individual and collective life.

It is this idea of Rita which lay behind the governing ideas that determined the organization of the varied aspects of life in India. Fundamentally, it gave rise to the predominant tendency to place the law of the truth as the sole law to which the individual and the collectivity are called upon to give their ultimate allegiance. Thus there came about in India an organization of human life in which each individual and collectivity was given the freedom to develop in accordance with the law of the truth; even the state authorities could legislate, but the legislation itself had to be in accordance with and in subservience to the law of the truth. This is what is meant by the law of Dharma and this is significance of the superiority that was ascribed to Dharma in determining the individual and collective life.

It is true that, according to the Vedic Rishis, Rita had to be discovered by each individual and that Rita could not be formulated in the form of rigid law. There are, however, certain universal harmonies, which once discovered, could become guidelines of action for those who had not yet directly experienced the Truth-Consciousness. These guidelines were to be found in the Veda itself, and they were expressed, tacitly or explicitly, as revelations and given to people in their varying capacities of receptivity as direct lines of approach to the truth either through a discipline or spiritual practice or through symbolism or through significant ritualism of the sacrifice. Thus there was no one uniform formulation of the law of the harmonies, and yet, there was a kind of coordination and an ascending gradation laid down for a progressive approach to the right law of action.

It is from this complex scheme and formulation that the later idea of Dharma grew and developed. As the original idea of Rita could never be rigidly fixed, even so, there could not be in India any one fixed formulation of Dharma. In a certain sense, Dharma has always remained some indefinable thing. Thus although Dharma has been upheld as the highest non-legislative law which even the highest state authorities had to obey, there is no where in India one fixed and uniform formulation of Dharma. Indeed, there have been several formulations and in many respects these formulations themselves have been in conflict with each other, and there are attempts even to reconcile this conflict resulting in some new flexible and synthetic formulation of law. From this complexity of the situation, there has arisen in India some universal and general idea of Dharma and certain recognized variations of the formulations of Dharma. The great *Smritis* of Yajnavalkya and Manu are attempts to codify this Dharma, and although these two are themselves in conflict with each other in many respects, they have provided a general background of a common formulation of the basic idea of Dharma. But this codification itself was never regarded as absolute, and although in later times they came to be applied rigidly, there were always supervening claims of the unformulated Dharma. In fact, we find in most catholic teachings such as those of the Gita an injunction to transcend all Dharmas and to surrender to the highest Truth and to the Supreme Divine.

Dharma is indeed a law or a guideline to prevent human beings from falling into *crooked* ways of the ordinary and unbridled demands of impulses, desires, ambitions and egoisms. That is why, Indian culture enjoined upon individuals to restrain the life of desire for enjoyment and for personal profit under the control of the uplifting law of Dharma. Thus we find in India, the prevalent idea that *Kama* and *Artha,* passion and personal gain are only the first elementary motives of life for the ordinary man and that they are not to be ends in themselves. *Kama* and *Artha* are to be superseded by *Dharma*. The individual is asked to grow out of passions and impulses and his selfish and egoistic interests to reach the life of ideal law of Dharma.

But even Dharma is not, according to Indian culture, the highest stage or motive of human life. For Dharma itself is not something fixed or rigid. And even if the initial stages of the pursuit of Dharma are guided by some fixed and acceptable code of conduct and action and behavior, the individual has to discover *Swadharma,* one's own specific law of the right rhythm of self-development. For Indian culture recognizes that every individual has his *own* specific dharma, the peculiar and individual law of the rhythm of his growth appropriate to his own individual functions and special combinations of his qualities and capacities. Thus the life of Dharma has to be a life of inner search, a life of self-knowledge. And when one begins to deal with himself, he discovers series of rhythms and ascending lines of Dharma. The individual is asked and allowed by the Indian culture to follow his swadharma to its own extreme limit, and at the height of this pursuit the individual discovers the real truth of himself, the true spiritual stuff of himself and also the true spiritual way of action, which cannot be bound by any previously formulated law of Dharma. This is the inner meaning of spiritual liberation, or *moksha,* which is placed before the individual as the superior or supreme aim of life.

There was a period in Indian history when the insistence on Dharma and the insistence on spiritual liberation as the higher and highest motive of life was at its peak. Such was the period that we find described in the Ramayana and Mahabharata. In later period, this insistence became weakened. But it was never entirely lost. It is true that the idea of Dharma itself became distorted and ill-conceived, and came to be imposed rigidly upon people and upon castes with some kind of brutality and intolerance. Thus, the inner kernel of Dharma, its inspiring force, its subtlety and its flexibility—all these suffered. But there always remained a deeper idea of Dharma available to individuals and communities who dared to revolt against the limiting and falsifying impositions of ill-conceived Dharma.

It must be admitted that the concept of Dharma although derived from the Vedic concept of Rita, was nonetheless its diminution, and it was inevitable that it could not remain for long a dynamic ideal. It broke down much earlier in the field of collective life, and even though it still continues to be respected and even practised to some extent by individuals in their individual life, it has betrayed its weaknesses and self-contradictions since the last several centuries. And under the impact of foreign invasions, particularly since the British introduced and imposed upon India the commercial scheme of values, there has arisen a tremendous confusion. In the renascent India there has been a new search and even attempts to revive the old scheme of values and of Dharma, but they are not found to be relevant and applicable to the present conditions.

This is where India is today. It is able neither to leave its old image nor to cast itself perilously in the image of the modern West. It is a state of suffocation, and yet the inertia inherited by it since the last several centuries is so great that there is not even a sufficient effort emerging from this suffocation.

This condition cannot last long, and we are forced to ask if the solution lies, not in return to Dharma, but in returning to the original Rita. But there is also a deeper question as to whether there was any special reason which necessitated the deviation or diminution of Rita at early stage of our history into Dharma, and later on into its fall. The question is if this special reason does not hold good even today. Or else it could be that the Vedic Rita itself was not sufficiently explored and fixed in life with sufficient knowledge and force. If so, there is an urgent need not only to rediscover the Rita but also to explore some new lines which still remained untraced in the past. In some such effort seems to be an answer to the smothering crisis of the present-day India.

11

Dharma and Fourfold Social Order

An important feature of the organization of Indian life was the complex and subtle arrangement of human life through four orders of communal life and four stages of individual life.

The human life was conceived as a process of gradual growth, and provisions came to be made in each stage of growth so as to stabilize that stage and to lead it gradually to the next higher stage. Thus, four major stages came to be recognized and each stage was presented with a set of ideals to be pursued and fulfilled. Each stage had its own *dharma*. These four, namely, *brahmacharya* (continence of student life), *grihastha* (balance of enjoyment and performance of duties appropriate to the householder), the *vanaprastha* (the preparation to leave ordinary life by enlargement, by travel, and by detachment, symbolized by dwelling in the forest), and *sanyasa* (final renunciation of ordinary life for the exclusive pursuit of spiritual life), were conceived as psychological stages of a large and flexible framework for the growth of the individual. And the general conditions of social life were so organized as to provide to each individual the necessary help needed by him at a given stage of his growth. This was further facilitated by the recognition of four types of temperaments among people with corresponding social functions, resulting in four divisions of the people in a composite social life. These four, the *Brahmin* (with the temperament that seeks knowledge and fulfills itself in the function of the teacher), the *Kshatirya* (with the temperament of power, courage, action and heroism which fulfills itself in the function of the ruler and the administrator), the *Vaishya* (with the temperament of mutuality, harmony and inter-change that fulfills itself in the function of commerce and inter-relationships), and *Shudra* (with the temperament of technical skill, service and physical labor), were the recognized types, each one requiring a stable field of education, experience and expression. Each type had its own *dharma*, and each had the suitable means of growth not only within its own limits, but also beyond to rise higher to the next ascending type of temperament and function. This was the original idea of *varna*, and at a certain stage of human civilization, this system provided not only psychological satisfaction but also some kind of a harmonious functioning of the social whole.

At the root of all this lay the original distinction made by the Vedic Rishis between the initiate and the non-initiate, between the one who was fit to receive the secret knowledge and revelation and the one who was too gross to receive the secrets of initiation. The Vedic Rishis recognised that the human being needs preparation before he can bear higher knowledge and culture. To prepare the individual was itself a subtle art of eduction, and the educator himself has to be the one who is not only an initate but also the accomplished, the *Siddha*, the *Rishi*. The important idea that developed in Vedic system of education was that of *adhikara*. *Adhikara* meant a special qualification to receive education and traning at a given stage of development which would also be appropriate for the preparation to rise to the next higher stage of development. Thus the higher knowledge could be imparted only to those who had the necessary qualification or *adhikara* for it. But there was also a recognition of the possibilities for each individual to obtain higher and higher stages of adhikara by means of self-development and self-culture. In the original Vedic concept, there was no rigidity and no final prohibition against any one in the pursuit of the highest knowledge. It only underlined the need for gradual development, balanced development, and comprehensive development.

The original concept of the *chaturvarna* (four orders) was in the Veda symbolic and spiritual. The Purusha Sukta of the Veda speaks of the four orders as having sprung from the body of the creative Deity (Purusha), - from his head, arms, thighs and legs. In the Vedic idea, the four orders represented the Divine in four aspects, the Divine as knwoeledge, the Divine as power, the Divine as production, enjoyment and mutulality, and the Divine as service, obedience and work.

In later times, however, there did enter rigidities and prohibitions and the whole system ultimately declined into rigid classifications and into codes of privileges and prohibitions. The Ashram system (the system of stages of life) broke down much earlier, the varna system (the system of classification in society) continued a little longer, but it began to crystallise itself and gradually degraded itself into a rigid caste system.

The caste system is still persistent. It is true that this system has come to be regarded as pernicious and injurious to the individual and to the society, and attempts have been made to get rid of this system, but there has been much failure.

Attempts are sometimes made to replace the caste system by the original and flexible system of varnas, but they too do not seem to hold out any promise of success.

Modern times are fast and there is in every field an accelerated speed of development. The society has, therefore, to be developed on lines on which accelerated growth as also integrated growth are facilitated to the maximum. This requires a new social organisation not developed at any time in human history. The survival or revival of the past is neither desirable nor practicable. Even according to the Indian theory, the system of varna (classification of society into fourfold order) does not belong either to the periods of man's highest attainment or to the eras of his lowest possibility. It is neither the principle of his ideal age of the perfected Truth nor of his iron age (called in Indian terminology *Kaliyuga*). In other words, the varna system is appropriate only to the intermediate ages of man's cycle in which he attempts to maintain some *imperfect form* of his true law. There are at least two such intermediate ages recognised by the Indian sociologists. They are called the *Treta* and the *Dwapara*. In the former, the social order is maintained by will power and force of character, and in the latter, by law, arrangement and fixed convention. In both these ages, man is developed and educated by fixing and emphasising the general prominent part of his active nature. But this does not aim at the education and development of the *integral man*. And as soon as those intermediate ages are crossed, as in the present age, there is a constant pressure for the accelerated and integrated growth of man. It is true that the present age makes upon man this demand by creating states of disorders or anarchy of our being. Nonetheless, the demand is clear and it can be fulfilled only by an attempt at a new order in which each individual is given opportunities and facilities to develop on his own line of development towards his *integral fullness*.

It is clear, therefore, that what is needed today, not only in India but everywhere else too, is a radical attempt at a *new* order.

In any case, Indian culture has reached a stage where what is needed is not a revival of the past, but a radical renewal.

In this process of renewal what was pre-figured in the Vedic wisdom of the need to perceive the Spirit in Matter and Matter in Spirit can and will undoubtedly play a major role. But what was pre-figured in the Veda needs not only to be rediscovered but also experimented upon by a new and potent wisdom, if there is to be a new birth of Indian culture. There is thus the imperative need to seek deeper and newer wisdom. And this seems to be the inevitable line of the immediate development of Indian culture.

12

Spirituality and Indian Culture

The history of India would remain enigmatic, particularly, the remarkable phenomenon of the continuity of Indian culture through the millennia would remain a mystery, if we do not take into account the role that spirituality has played not only in determining the direction of her philosophical and cultural effort but also in replenishing the springs of creativity at every crucial hour in the long and often weary journey. It is true that spirituality has played a role in every civilization and that no culture can claim a monopoly for spirituality. And yet, it can safely be affirmed that the unique greatness and continuity of Indian culture can be traced to her unparalleled experimentation, discovery and achievement in the vast field of spirituality.

Indian culture has recognized spirituality not only as the supreme occupation of man but also as his all-integrating occupation. Similarly, the entire spectrum of Indian culture,—its religion, ethics, philosophy, literature, art, architecture, dance, music, and even its polity and social and economic organization,—all these have been constantly influenced and moulded by the inspiring force of a multi-sided spirituality.

The distinctive character of Indian spirituality is its conscious and deliberate insistence on *direct experience.* It affirms that deep within the heart and high above the mind there is accessible to our consciousness a realm of truths, powers and ecstasies that we can, by methodised effort of Yoga*, realize in direct experience, can even hold permanently, and express in varying degrees through our instruments of the mind, life and body. This affirmation has

*Yoga is a comprehensive system of concentration, passive and dynamic, leading to living contact, union and identity with realities or Reality underlying the universe, with appropriate consequences in our nature and action, individual and cosmic. In recent times, Yoga is often misrepresented to be identical with Hathayoga, a system of physical and subtle exercises, which is only a specialisation, and a dispensable one, of the real comprehensive system.

conditioned the entire development of religion in India and has introduced in the body of religion the recognition that direct experience of the spirit is far superior to dogma, belief and ritualism, and that *dogmatic religion* can and must ultimately be surpassed by *experiential spirituality*.

Consequently, the history of Indian spirituality and religion shows a remarkable spirit of research, of an increasing subtlety, plasticity, sounding of depths, extension of seeking. There have been systems of specialization and also conflicting claims and counter-claims, but the supervening tendency has been to combine, assimilate, harmonize and synthesize. In the past, there have been at least four great stages of synthesis, represented by the Vedas, the Upanishads, the Gita, and the Tantra. And, in modern times, we are passing through the fifth stage, represented by a new synthesis, which is in the making.

It is impossible to describe Indian spirituality and religion by any exclusive label. Even in its advanced forms, it cannot be described as monotheism or monism or pantheism or nihilism or transcendtalism, although each one of these is present in it in some subtle or pronounced way. Even the spiritual truths behind the primitive forms such as those of animism, spiritism, fetishism and totemism have been allowed to play a role in its complex totality, although their external forms have been discouraged and are not valid or applicable to those who lead an inner mental and spiritual life. It is this complexity that bewilders the foreign student when he tries to define Indian spirituality and religion in terms and under criteria that are not born of the Indian experiment. But things become easier once it is grasped that the fundamental point of reference is not the outward form of a given belief and practice but the spirit behind and the justifying spiritual experience.

Indian scriptures and records abound with the statements and descriptions of varieties of spiritual experience. But there are three central spiritual experiences in terms of which all these varieties can be readily understood. The first is that of the individual in a state of complete detachment from all movement, dynamism, activity. In this state, the individual finds himself in an utter passivity and inactivity, but also of a complete luminosity and discrimination between himself as an eternal witness *(sakshin)*, free from the sense of ego and the activities of Nature in the universe. This experience is the basis of the *Sankhya* philosophy. The second experience is that of the eternal and infinite Reality above Space and Time in which all that we call individuality and universality are completely silenced and sublated, and the experiencing consciousness discovers itself to be That Reality *(tat sat)*, one, without the second *(ekam eva advitiyam)*, entirely silent and immobile, the Pure Being, so ineffable that even to describe it as Being is to violate its sheer transcendence. This experience has given rise to the philosophy of *Adwaita* (Non-Dualism), in particular that of Illusionistic Adwaita, which proclaims that only the Brahman is real, and the world is an illusion. The third experience is the one in which the individual and cosmos are found to be free expressions of the Supreme Reality *(Purushottama)* which, although above Space and Time, determines Space and Time and all activities through various intermediary expressions of itself. This experience and some variations of it form the basis of various theistic philosophies of India. These theistic philosophies are those of qualified monism *(Vishishtadwaita philosophy)*, integral monism *(Poornadwaita philosophy)*, dualiatic philosophy *(Dwaita philosophy)*. These experiences, when permanently established give liberation (moksha), and it is this which has in India been regarded as a high consummation of man's destiny upon earth. But, more importantly, the ancient ideal as given by the Vedas, Upanishads and the Gita, was to achieve an integrality of all these experiences, to combine utter Silence with effective Action, to be liberated from ego and yet at the same time to be a free living centre *(jivanmukta)* of luminous action that would aid the progressive unity of mankind *(lokasangraha)*.

This integral ideal was to be realized in its integrality not only by a few exceptional individuals but also by increasing number of people, groups, collectivities, even on massive scale, through a long and conscious preparation and training. This great and difficult task has passed through two main stages, while a third has taken initial steps and promises to be the destiny of India's future.

The early Vedic was the first stage; the Purano-Tantric was the second stage*. In the former, an attempt was made to approach the mass-mind through the physical mind of man and make it familiar

*The date of the Vedic age is controversial, but according to a conservative hypothesis, its origins are dated 2000 B.C The Purano-Tantric age can be regarded to have extended from 600 B.C. to 800 B.C

with the Godhead in the universe through the symbol of the sacrificial fire *(yajna)*. In the latter, deeper approaches of man's inner mind and life to the Divine in the universe were attempted through the development of great philosophies,* many-sided epic literature (particularly Ramayana and Mahabharata), systems of Puranas and Tantras,** and even art and science. An enlarged secular turn was given, and this was balanced by deepening of the intensities of psycho-religious experience. New tendencies and mystic forms and disciplines attempted to seize not only the soul and the intellect, but the emotions, the senses, the vital and the aesthetic nature of man and turn them into stuff of the spiritual life. But this great effort and achievement which covered all the time between the Vedic age and the decline of Buddhism, was still not the last possibility of the spiritual and religious evolution open to Indian culture. A further development through the third stage was attempted, but it was arrested as it synchronized with a period of general exhaustion, and, in the eighteenth century, which can be regarded as the period of dense obscurity, the work that had begun seemed almost lost.

The aim of this third stage was to approach not only the inner mind and life of man, but to approach his whole mental, psychical and physical living, his totality of being and activity, and to turn it into a first beginning of at least a *generalized* spiritual life. Philosophers and saints such as Sri Chaitanya (1485-1533) and others of the 15th and 16th centuries belong to this stage. There

*Particularly, the six systems, *Nyaya, Vaisheshika, Sankhya, Yoga, Poorva Mimamsa and Uttara Mimamsa* and their numerous interpretations and commentaries. These 6 systems are Vedic systems of philosophy. There developed also Buddhism and Jainism and their numerous philosophical systems which did not accept the authority of the Vedas. Similarly, Charvaka philosophy, the philosophy of materialism, which also developed during this period, was entirely anti-Vedic.

**There are 18 Puranas. Each Purana has five parts: (1) creation of the world, (2) destruction and recreation of the world, (3) reigns and periods of Manus, (4) geneology and Gods, and (5) dynasties of solar and lunar kings.

While Puranas are Vedic, Tantras are Vedic only indirectly, and they are called *Agamas*. We do not know the exact number of *Agamas*, but it is estimated that there are 64 of them.

Tantras are devoted to the methods of utilising the dynamic energies of life in order to open up the doors of the Divine Power for a triumphant mastery over the world-activities.

was also during this period a remarkable attempt to combine Vedanta and Islam or of establishing lasting communal harmony. In particular, the work of Guru Nanak (1469-1538) and of the subsequent Sikh Khalsa movement was astonishingly original and novel. The speciality of this third stage was an intense outburst and fresh creativity, *not a revivalism*, but based upon a deep assimilation of the past, a new effort and a new formulation. But the time was not yet ripe, and India had to pass through a period of an eclipse, almost total and disastrous.

Happily, the 19th century witnessed a great awakening and a new spiritual impulse pregnant with a power to fulfill the mission of the work that had started in the third stage. Great and flaming pioneers appeared, Raja Rammohan Roy (1836-1886) and Swami Vivekananda (1862-1902) - to name just two of them -, and through their work the entire country was electrified not only spiritually but even socially and politically. India became renascent, and there began to develop a capacity for a new synthesis, not only of the threads of Indian culture but also of world culture. Nationalism came to be proclaimed as the new spirituality, and this nationalism was right from the beginning international in its spirit and sweep. Not an escape from life, but acceptance of life, integration of life and transformation of life by an integral spirituality - this ideal came to be felt and expressed in various ways and through various activities of the renascent India.

Gradually, it has become evident that this new movement has to do not merely with India but fundamentally with the essential problem of Man and his future evolution. It is becoming clearer that Man is a field of interaction between Matter and Spirit, that this interaction has reached a point of *criticality*, and that this criticality demands a new knowledge, an integral knowledge of Matter and Spirit.

This is the task which Free India has begun to perceive as central to her real fulfillment. It is significant that we have in India a most comprehensive statement of this task in the luminous writings of Sri Aurobindo (1872-1950), who has been described by Romain Rolland as 'the completest synthesis of the East and the West'. Sri Aurobindo has declared that man is a transitional being, that his destiny is to be the spiritual superman, and that the present hour is the hour of his evolutionary crisis in which his entire life, his very body, must undergo an integral spiritual transformation, not indeed by an escape into some far-off heavens, but here, in this physical earth itself, by a victorious union of Spirit and Matter. This, he has declared, is not an issue of an individual but of collectivity, not an issue of Indian spirituality and culture, but of the entire world's upward aspiration and fulfillment.

It must be noted that in this task of universal importance, India, the East, has received from the West a collaboration of incalculable magnitude and value. For it is from France that the Mother (Madame Mira Alfassa (1878-1973) came to Sri Aurobindo and made India her permanent home in order to collaborate with him and to fulfill this task of integral transformation. The work that she has done is not yet sufficiently known, but we find in her the highest heights that Indian spirituality has reached, and we feel that the near future will show the revolutionary effects of her work for humanity, for its lasting unity and harmony, and for its transmutation into super-humanity.

Indeed the renascent spirituality of India opens up new vistas of experience and research. It transcends the boundaries of dogma and exclusive claims of Truth. It is not opposed to any religion, but points to a way to a synthesis and integrality of spiritual experience in the light of which the truth behind each religion is understood and permitted to grow to its fullness and to meet in harmony with all the others. The important thing is to turn the human mentality, vitality and physicality to the realm of spiritual experiences and to transform the human mould by an over-widening light of the Spirit. In this perception, even scepticism, agnosticism and atheism have a meaning and value as an indispensable stage for a certain line of mental development. But here too the dogma and denial behind the doubt and atheism have to be surpassed, and whether by rigorous methods of philosophy and science or by a deeper plunge into deeper experiences, a way can be opened to transcend the dogmatic refusal to seek and to discover. It is in this direction that we seem to reach a point where a fruitful synthesis of science and spirituality can be effectuated.

The renascent spirituality is all-embracing and is deeply committed to undertake all activities of human life and to transform them. It has begun to influence literature and art and music, education and physical culture. Even social and economic and political fields are being taken up, not indeed to cast them once again into some rigid formula of a religious dogma but rather to liberate them and to inundate them with a spiritual light and motive and to restructure them by a gradual evolution so that they may breathe widely and freely the progressive harmonies of Liberty, Equality and Fraternity. Thus is it that the old forms of society, casteism and all the rest, are being broken and there is a fresh search for new forms, plastic and flexible, to permit the highest possible perfectibility of the individual and the collectivity to blossom spontaneously and perpetually. In the ultimate analysis, it is through such a vast and potent change in the social milieu that the total man can be uplifted to his next stage of evolutionary mutation.

It is in this context that India views the great social-political upheavals of the recent times as a sign and a promise of the coming of the New World. It views modern man's concern for the collective life as something unprecedented. The experiments that have been heralded by the great revolutions have contributed to the re-making of the collective life of Man. It is felt that these experiments will continue to grow until the highest and the deepest in the individual and the collectivity are brought forward in the task of the new transformation. It is in this direction that the new spirituality seems to be moving. It is in this direction that the new philosophies are likely to flower. India has already taken this new direction and it hopes to place the fruits of this new endeavor at the service of mankind for its highest welfare.

Appendix I

The Rishi and the Brahmacharin

In ancient India, the concept of the Rishi connoted the highest ideal of the teacher. The teacher was a Yogin, one who had realized or was a seeker of true knowledge that comes through the practice of Yoga, which was at that time a developing science and art of psychological concentration and perfection. The Vedic Rishis described their aspirations and victories in the form of Mantra, inevitable expression born out of innermost vision and realization.

The Vedic Rishis refer to their 'forefathers' as great pathfinders, and spoke of them in legends and myths in order to describe what they had achieved. For example, Parashara says: 'Our fathers broke open the firm and strong places by their words, yea, the Angirasas broke open the hill by their cry; they made in us the path to the great heaven; they found the Day and Swar and vision and the luminous Cows' (1.71.2). This path, he tells us, is the path which leads to immortality, 'They who entered into all things that bear right fruit formed a path towards immortality; earth stood wide for them by the greatness and by the Great Ones, the mother Aditi with her sons came (or, manifested herself) for the upholding' (1.72.9). The meaning of these cryptic verses is that the physical being is visited by the greatness of the infinite planes above and by the power of the great godheads who reign on those planes. This breaks the limits of the physical being, which opens out to the Light and is upheld in its new wideness by the infinite Consciousness, mother Aditi, and her sons, the divine powers of the supreme Deva or Lord. This was the meaning of Vedic immortality.

There are also references in the second hymn of the fourth Mandala to the seven divine seers, who are the divine Angirasas and the human fathers. Riks 12 to 15 describe the seven Rishis as the supreme ordainers of the world-sacrifice, and put forth the idea of the human being 'becoming' the seven Rishis, that is to say, creating them in himself and growing into that which they mean, just as he becomes the Heaven and Earth and the other gods; or, as it is otherwise put, man begets or creates or forms the divine birth in his own being. As Rik 15 says: 'Now as the seven seers of Dawn, the Mother, the supreme disposers [of sacrifice, which in psychological terms means self-consecration, the discipline by which the separative sense of egoism is destroyed], may we beget for ourselves the gods; may we become the Angirasas, sons of Heaven breaking open the wealth-filled hill, shining in purity.' These Riks bring out the idea of the human fathers as the original type of the great becoming and achievement.

The word Veda is derived from the root vid, to know, and the Vedic Rishis looked upon the Veda as the Book of Knowledge. The Vedic Rishis discovered that the secret of victory lies in aspiration, which expresses itself in the form of burning flame, Agni. This burning flame rises higher and higher in our being, destroying impurities and obscurities, and there arise in us king-ideas, master-wills, intense prayers. There is then a response, and the doors of secret knowledge and power swing open giving birth to creative action or event. Victory is achieved - our being with its imperfect thought, will and emotion, is filled with vastness, luminosity and unfailing energy. The immortal in us is realized and becomes manifest.

The Veda contains the secrets of this realization. It is the science and art of the inter-relationship of our earthly being with the powers around it and above it, and of the processes by which our imperfections can be remedied. The Veda is indeed a book of discoveries, a record of research that the ancient fathers and their initiates carried on by personal verification, rediscovery and constant enlargement.

One of the most important legends of the Veda is the legend of the Angirasas. Its theme is the spiritual life of man but, to make it concrete to themselves and while veiling its secrets from the unfit, the Vedic poets expressed it in poetic images drawn from outward life. The Angirasas are pilgrims of the lights. They are those who travel towards the goal and attain to the highest, 'they who travel to and attain that supreme treasure' (II.24.6). Their action is invoked for carrying the life of man farther towards its goal. The journey is principally the quest of the hidden light, but through the opposition of the powers of darkness it also becomes an expedition and a battle. The Angirasas are heroes and fighters of that battle, 'fighters for the cows or rays of light and knowledge' (goshu yodhah). They discover the supraphysical power or being, the king of the kingdom of illumined intelligence (Swar), and they seek his help. This being is Indra, who marches with them (saranyubhih), travellers on the path(sakhibhih), comrades, seers and singers of the sacred chant, and fighters in the battle. Strengthened by them he conquers during the journey and reaches the goal. The journey proceeds along the path discovered by Sarama, the hound of heaven, the intuitive power that sees that path directly, the path of the Truth, *ritasya panthah,* the great path, *mahas panthah,* which leads to the realms of the Truth.

The drinking of the soma wine as the means of strength, victory and attainment is one of the pervading figures of the Veda. The soma wine is the sweetness that comes flowing from the streams of the hidden upper world, it is that which flows in the seven waters, it is that with which the ghrita, the clarified butter of the mystic sacrifice, is instinct, it is the honeyed wave which rises out of the ocean of life. Such images, as pointed out by Sri Aurobindo, can have only one meaning: 'It is the divine delight hidden in all existence which once manifest, supports all life's crowning activities and is the force that finally immortalizes the mortal, the amritam, ambrosia of the gods.' The Angirasas are distinguished by their seerhood, Rishihood. They are the fathers who are full of the soma, they have the word and are increasers of the Truth. The Angirasas have been described as those who speak rightly, masters of the Rik who place perfectly their thought; they are heroes who speak the truth and think with straightness and thus are able to hold the seat of illumined knowledge (*vide* Rig Veda, X.67.2).

The ancient Indian idea of the teacher is conceived in the light of the image of the Angirasas, and it is for this reason that the teacher came to be placed so supreme. The verses we have presented here give only a few glimpses of the aspirations and achievements of the ancient teachers.

The meanings of the Vedic verses are not fully understandable; therefore, a great deal of research is required to discover the secret of the Veda. To understand exactly what the Vedic Rishis achieved, the reader may refer to Sri Aurobindo's luminous interpretation in The Secret of the Veda.

The verses we have chosen below are hymns addressed to Agni, a word which is translated as power, strength, will, the god-will, or the Flame according to the context. The Veda speaks of Agni, the divine Flame, in a series of splendid and opulent images. He is the rapturous priest of the sacrifice, the young sage, the sleepless envoy, the ever-wakeful flame in the house, the master of our gated dwelling-place, the beloved guest, the divine child, the pure and virgin god, the invincible warrior, the leader on the path who marches in front of the human peoples, the immortal in mortals, the worker established in man by the gods, the unobstructed in knowledge, the infinite in being, the vast and flaming sun of the Truth, the sustainer of the sacrifice and discerner of its steps, the divine perception, the Light, the vision, the firm foundation. We experience Agni as our upward aspiration, the will towards Truth, and the force that uplifts us from our limitations by renunciation, purification and right enjoyment. This aspiration, when it reaches its acme, is what brings to us the victory—deliverance from falsehood into Truth, from darkness into Light, from death into immortality.

One of the great discoveries of the Vedic Rishis was the knowledge of the hierarchy of the various worlds and the inter-relationship and interaction of the physical world with the supraphysical worlds. Based on this knowledge, they found and applied the means by which man in the physical world can attain perfection. In their system of knowledge, Agni is found to be the fundamental bridge between the lower and the higher, a messenger that travels and turns human aspiration into divine victory, a will that enables man to rise above human limitations so as to become a candidate for perfection.

The Vedas were followed by the Brahmanas and Aranyakas. While the Brahmanas dealt with the ritualistic aspects of the Veda, the Aranyakas brought out the inner meaning of the teachings of the Rishis. The Aranyakas were followed by the Upanishads. The word Upanishad consists of three components, upa, ni and shad, where shad means to dwell, upa means near and ni means closer. Thus Upanishad means dwelling very closely to the secret knowledge. Upanishads are also regarded as Vedanta, which means the end of the Veda. The Rishis of the Upanishads attempted to recover the Vedic knowledge which had become obscured in the course of time. The language of the Upanishads is much clearer than that of the Veda, even though it has yielded to various interpretations.

There are more than two hundred Upanishads. But the principal Upanishads are between eight and twelve. Isa, Kena, Katha,

Prashna, Chhandogya, Brihadaranyaka, Mundaka, Mandukya, Taittiriya and Shvetashvatara are the most prominent. The stories that we have selected below for this book are taken from the Chhandogya Upanishad and Katha Upanishad.

The Upanishads give us a clear idea of the ancient system of education and of the role of the teacher and the pupil. Some of the examples that are given here clearly indicate that the pupil was supposed to approach the teacher and seek instruction from him, that the good teacher judged the pupil by his truthfulness and the earnestness of his seeking, and that the good pupil was the one who chose the path of the good rather than that of the pleasant. The Upanishads also point out that the knowledge sought by the teachers and pupils was the knowledge that transcends appearances and seizes upon Reality through direct experience.

In the story of Satyakama, we have an illustration of a young student who has an ardent aspiration to learn and study. His first quality is truthfulness, and the teacher rightly accepts him, convinced that his truthfulness is sufficient evidence of his qualification to be admitted.

In the next story, taken from the Katha Upanishad, we have Nachiketas, a young brahmacharin, who is offered by his father to Yama, the god who controls and governs the kingdom of death. We are told that Nachiketas, seeing his father giving away old cows as offerings to Brahmins, feels that his father ought to give something valuable and asks his father to whom he (Nachiketas) should be given as a sacrifice and offering. Thrice he asks his father, and his father, annoyed with his insistence, pronounces that he is offered to Yama. The young Nachiketas visits the abode of Yama, where he waits for three days for Yama's arrival. When Yama comes, he is pleased with Nachiketas for his patience and sincerity, and offers him three boons. Nachiketas first asks for his father's appeasement and his well-being, which Yama grants readily. Next, he asks for the knowledge of the secret of the fire of austerity. And, lastly he asks for the knowledge of the secret of death, of what happens to man after death and what really is the secret of immortality. Yama does not intend to give away this secret and offers him the choice of worldly happiness in the form of riches and progeny and success. However, Nachiketas is firm in his demand and rejects the choice offered by Yama. Yama is pleased with the steadfast adherence of Nachiketas to his noble search, and grants him the secret knowledge. The short extract presented here in this book is a dialogue between Yama and Nachiketas, in which Yama explains the distinction between the good and the pleasant, and points out that since Nachiketas chose the good in preference to the pleasant, he considers Nachiketas a worthy pupil who deserves to be given the secret knowledge.

The third story, taken from the Chhandogya Upanishad, contains a famous dialogue between Aruni and his son, Shvetaketu. There are three important elements in the extract. In the first place, we have here an illustration of the method of teaching by dialogue and personal experimentation. Secondly, the central question raised by Aruni is one of the most striking questions that every good teacher and pupil should raise: 'What is it knowing which everything is known?' Thirdly, the answer provided to the question is perhaps the quintessence of India's entire approach to the problem of knowledge. In brief the answer is that the knowledge of essence gives us the foundation of all that is manifested, and that the quintessence of all phenomena is the inner self which is identical with that which transcends all and manifests all. Tat tvam asi, 'thou art That', is one of the great pronouncements of the Upanishadic knowledge, and Aruni explains this knowledge by various examples, so that the pupil can grasp it.

In modern times, science, after its triumphant discoveries and inventions, is slowly returning to the realization that knowledge depends very much on the knower, and that the most important object of knowledge is the self that is seeking knowledge. Schrodinger and others have come to the conclusion that this new orientation will press the scientific inquiry into the field of self-knowledge. Here we see the modern quest converging on the ancient wisdom.

In the fourth story, which is also taken from the Chhandogya Upanishad, we have a dialogue between Narada and Sanatkumara. When Narada approaches Sanatkumara, Sanatkumara says: 'Tell me what you already know; then I will impart to you what lies outside it.' Narada replies enumerating a large number of disciplines of knowledge that he has already learned. Sanatkumara points out that what Narada knows is only name and that there is something greater than name. This brings out the real distinction between learning and knowledge. The aim of the good teacher is to help the pupil liberate himself from the cobwebs of learning and to lead him to the luminosity of true knowledge.

In connection with the story of Narada and Sanatkumara, it may be worth noting that ancient India had developed a wide variety of disciplines of the sciences and arts. It is difficult to say whether these disciplines developed during the Upanishadic age, but to some extent they surely did, and we have some information about the curriculum followed in Taxila, the most important seat of learning in ancient India. It is said that Taxila was founded by Bharata and named after his son Taksha, who was established there as ruler. (Taxila was situated about twenty miles west of modern Rawalpindi.) Apart from the Vedic knowledge, grammar, philosophy, and eighteen shilpas were the principal subjects of specialization. It is surmised that these eighteen shilpas were as follows: vocal music, instrumental music, dancing, painting, mathematics, accounting, engineering, sculpture, agriculture, cattle-breeding, commerce, medicine, conveyancing and law, administrative training, archery and military art, magic, snake-charming and poison antidotes, the art of finding hidden treasures.

Later literature mentions sixty-four Kalas, which a cultured lady was expected to master. These included the art of cooking, skill in the use of body ointments and paints for the teeth, etc., music, dancing, painting, garland-making, floor decoration, preparation of the bed, proper use and care of dress and ornaments, sewing, elementary carpentry, repair of household tools and articles, reading, writing and understanding different languages, composing poems, understanding dramas, physical exercises, recreation for utilizing leisure hours, and the art of preparing toys for children.

In the Upanishadic literature we come to know of a large number of good teachers and good pupils. In the selection presented here, there are Satyakama Jabala, Nachiketas, Shvetaketu and Narada. We may also refer to the traditional story of Uddalaka Aruni, the son of Aruna Gautama and father of Shvetaketu. Most of the important works of the period refer to him as an authority on rituals and inner knowledge. As a pupil, he is often cited for his devotion to his teacher. He was asked by his teacher to prevent the inundation of the ashram farm during a rainy day. Unable to plug a crack in the dam, he used his own body to plug the breach and thus prevented the inundation of the farm. The Chhandogya

Upanishad makes reference to Krishna Devakiputra who received initiation and knowledge from his teacher, Ghora. He is indeed the one declared later to be the Lord Krishna. The Upanishads describe him as a student eager in his pursuit of knowledge. We may also mention Pippalada, a great sage in the Prashna Upanishad. Raikva is the name of the cart driver whom the King Janashruti approached for instruction. In the Brihadaranyaka Upanishad, we have a vivid account of the supremacy of Yajnavalkya. According to the story, Yajnavalkya's guru, Uddalaka Aruni, could not hold his own in a disputation with him in a vast assembly of scholars from the entire Kuru Panchala country which had been summoned by King Janaka of Videha. The Upanishads contain other great names of teachers and pupils, such as Ashvala, Jarat Karava Artabhiga, Bhujyu Lahyayani, Ushasti Chakrayana, Kahoda Kaushitakeya, and Gargi Vachaknavi. We should also mention Maitreyi, a learned wife of Yajnavalkya, who 'was conversant with Brahman'. One of the famous dialogues in the Brihadaranyaka Upanishad is between Yajnavalkya and Maitreyi. This dialogue occurs when Yajnavalkya is about to renounce the life of a householder for that of a hermit, and he proposes to divide his wealth between his two wives, Katyayani and Maitreyi. But Maitreyi insists on his giving her instruction in spiritual wisdom.

According to tradition, Dhaumya was a great teacher, and stories are told not only of Aruni Uddalaka, one of his good pupils to whom we have referred earlier, but also of his other pupil Veda, who is reported to have himself become a very good teacher. Veda is especially noted for the devotion displayed by one of his pupils, Utanka. On the completion of his studentship, Utanka encounters every sort of experience and danger in order to procure the presents of Veda's choice before being free to leave his preceptor's home.

Another picture of ideal studentship is brought out in the story of Kacha and Devayani. Devayani's father Sukracharya was Kacha's teacher. She fell in love with Kacha, but he had taken the vow of brahmacharya and refused to enter into marriage with her. One passage in the Mahabharata gives Kacha's description of the life he lived in that retreat of learning: 'Carrying the burden of sacrificial wood, kusha grass, and fuel, I was coming towards the hermitage and feeling tired, sat for rest under the banyan tree, along with my companions, the kine under my charge.' This brings out the fact that one of the traditional duties of the student was to tend his preceptor's cattle, and collect wood for fire and sacrifice, and this put him into intimate touch with Nature and subjected him to the influence and educational processes of Nature working through 'silent sympathy' as Wordsworth put it. The Mahabharata gives the full traditional story of Kacha and Devayani.

A number of books on the Upanishads are available. We have taken the extract from the Katha Upanishad from Sri Aurobindo's book *'The Upanishads.'* The other extracts are from the translation by V.M. Bedekar and G.B. Palsule.

Aspirations and Victories of the Ancient Rishis

(A few selections from the Rig Veda)*

I

(The Rishi desires a state of spiritual wealth full of the divine working in which nothing shall fall away to the division and the crookedness. So, increasing by our works the divine Force in us daily, we shall attain to the Bliss and the Truth, the rapture of the Light and the rapture of the Force.)

1. O Will,O conqueror of our plenitude, the felicity which thou alone canst conceive in the mind, that make full of inspiration by our words and set it to labor in the gods as our helper.

2. They who are powers increased of thee in the fierceness of thy flame and strength, yet impel us not on the path, they fall away to division, they cleave to the crookedness of a law that is other than thine.

3. Thee, O Will, we take to us as the priest of the offering and the accomplisher of a discerning knowledge; holding for thee all our delights we call thee the ancient and supreme to our sacrifices by the word.

4. Rightly and in such wise that, O forceful god, O perfect power of works, we may increase thee day by day, that we may have the Bliss, that we may have the Truth, that we may have perfect rapture by the Rays of the knowledge, that we may have perfect rapture by the Heroes of the Force.

Rig Veda V.20.1-4

II

(The Rishi celebrates the flame of the Will high-blazing in the dawn of knowledge as the King of Immortality, the giver to the

*These selections have been made from "The Secret of the Veda" by Sri Aurobindo.

soul of its spiritual riches and felicity and of a well-governed mastery of Nature. He is the bearer of our oblation, the illumined guide of our sacrifice to its divine and universal goal.)

1. The Flame of Will burning high rises to his pure light in the heaven of mind; wide he extends his illumination and fronts the Dawn. She comes, moving upward, laden with all desirable things, seeking the gods with the oblation, luminous with the clarity.

2. When thou burnest high thou art king of immortality and thou cleavest to the doer of sacrifice to give him that blissful state; he to whom thou comest to be his guest, holds in himself all substance and he sets thee within in his front.

3. O Flame, put forth thy battling might for a vast enjoyment of bliss; may there be thy highest illumination; create a well-governed union of the Lord and his Spouse, set thy foot on the greatness of hostile powers.

4. I adore, O Flame, the glory of thy high-blazing mightiness. Thou art the Bull with the illuminations; thou burnest up in the march of our sacrifices.

5. O Flame that receivest our offerings, perfect guide of the sacrifice, high-kindled offer our oblation to the godheads; for thou art the bearer of our offerings.

6. Cast the offering, serve the Will with your works while your sacrifice moves forward to its goal, accept the carrier of our oblation.

Rig Veda V.28.1-6

III

Vanished the darkness, shaken in its foundation; Heaven shone out (rocata dyauh, implying the manifestation of the three luminous worlds of Swar, diyo rocanani); upward rose the light of the divine Dawn; the Sun entered the vast fields (of the Truth) beholding the straight things and the crooked in mortals. Thereafter indeed they awoke and saw utterly (by the sun's separation of the straight from the crooked, the truth from falsehood); then indeed they held in them the bliss that is enjoyed in heaven.

Rig Veda. IV. 1. 17

May he the knower discern perfectly the Knowledge and the Ignorance, the wide levels and the crooked that shut in mortals; and, O God, for a bliss fruitful in offspring, lavish on us Diti and protect Aditi.

Rig Veda IV.2.11

Now as the seven seers of Dawn, the Mother, the supreme disposers (of the sacrifice), may we beget for ourselves the gods; may we become the Angirasas, sons of Heaven, breaking open the wealth-filled hill, shining in purity.

Rig Veda IV.2.15

We have done the work for thee, we have become perfect in works, the wide-shining Dawns have taken up their home in the Truth (or, have robed themselves with the Truth), in the fullness of Agni and his manifold delight, in the shining eye of the god in all his brightness.

Rig Veda IV.2.19

Brahmacharins in Search of Knowledge

(A few selections from the Upanishad)

I*

Truthfulness

1. Satyakama Jabala said to his Mother Jabala: 'Venerable mother: I wish to join school as a brahmacharin (pupil wishing to learn the true knowledge). Please tell me from what family I hail.'

2. She said to him: 'My child, I don't know from what family you are. In my youth, I went about in many places as a maid-servant; during that period I begot you; I myself do not know from what family you hail; I am called Jabala and you are called Satyakama; so call yourself then Satyakama, the son of Jabala.'

3. Then he went to Haridrumata Gautama and said: 'I wish to join your school, venerable Sir, as a Brahmacharin, if you, vernerable Sir, would desire to accept me.'

4. He said to him; 'My dear child, from what family do you hail?' He replied: "Venerable Sir, I do not know from what family I hail; I have asked my mother who answered me: 'In my youth, I went about in many places as a maid-servant; during that period I begot you. I myself don't know from what family you hail. I am called Jabala and you are called Satyakama.' Therefore I call myself Satyakama, son of Jabala, venerable Sir."

5. He (the preceptor) replied to him: 'Only a Brahmana can speak so candidly. My dear child, bring here the fuel-sticks (which are requisite for the ceremonial rite). I will accept you, because you have not swerved from truthfulness.'

After he had accepted him, he separated from the herd four hundred lean and weak cows and said: 'My dear, go after them and tend them.' Satyakama then drove them forth and said to his teacher: 'Not before they have become one thousand, will I return.' So he lived far away for a number of years.

Chhandogya Upanishad, Fourth Chapter, Fourth Part

*This passage is taken from the translation by V.M. Bedekar and G.B. Palsule.

II*

The Good and the Pleasant

Yama speaks:

1. 'One thing is the good and quite another thing is the pleasant, and both seize upon a man with different meanings. Of these who takes the good, it is well with him; he falls from the aim of life who chooses the pleasant.

2. 'The good and the pleasant come to a man and the thoughtful mind turns all around them and distinguishes. The wise chooses out the good from the pleasant, but the dull soul chooses the pleasant rather than the getting of his good and its having.

3. 'And thou, O Nachiketas, hast looked close at the objects of desire, at pleasant things and beautiful, and thou hast cast them from thee; thou hast not entered into the net of riches in which many men sink to perdition.

4. 'For far apart are these, opposite, divergent, the one that is known as the ignorance and the other the Knowledge. But Nachiketas I deem truly desirous of the knowledge whom so many desirable things could not make to lust after them.

5. 'They who dwell in the ignorance, within it, wise in their own wit and deeming themselves very learned, men bewildered are they who wander about stumbling round and round helplessly like blind men led by the blind.

6. 'The childish wit bewildered and drunken with the illusion of riches cannot open its eyes to see the passage to heaven: for he that thinks this world is and there is no other, comes again and again into Death's thraldom.

7. 'He that is not easy to be heard of by many, and even of those that have heard, they are many who have not known Him,—a miracle is the man that can speak of Him wisely or is skillful to win Him, and when one is found, a miracle is the listener who can know Him even when taught of Him by the knower.

*This passage is taken from *Upanishads* by Sri Aurobindo.

8. 'An inferior man cannot tell you of Him; for thus told thou canst not truly know Him, since He is thought of in many aspects. Yet unless told of Him by another thou canst not find thy way to Him; for He is subtler than subtlety and that which logic cannot reach.

9. 'This wisdom is not to be had by reasoning, O beloved Nachiketas; only when told thee by another it brings real knowledge,—the wisdom which thou hast gotten. Truly thou art steadfast in the Truth! Even such a questioner as thou art may I meet with always.'

Nachiketas speaks:

10. 'I know of treasure that it is not for ever; for not by things unstable shall one attain That One which is stable; therefore I heaped the fire of Nachiketas, and by the sacrifice of momentary things I won the Eternal.'

Katha Upanishad, First Cycle: Second Chapter 1-10

III*

What is it Knowing Which Everything Is Known?

1. Svetaketu was the son of (Uddalaka) Aruni. His father said to him: 'Svetaketu! Move and go to study the true Knowledge, because, my dear one, none of our family used to be unlearned and remain a mere appendage of Brahmanhood (a Brahman only in name).'

2. Then he, while twelve years of age, went as a pupil to a teacher and when he was twenty-four years old, had thoroughly studied all the books of Knowledge. He returned haughty in mind, conceited and thinking himself wise. Then his father said to him: 'O dear one! Since you are haughty in mind, conceited and consider yourself wise, have you inquired into that instruction whereby what is even unheard of, becomes heard, what is not comprehended becomes comprehended, what is not known becomes known?'

3. 'Venerable Sir, how is that instruction?'

'Just as, O dear one, through one lump of clay everything that consists of clay is known, modification being a clinging to words, only a name, it is only clay in reality.

4. 'Just as, O dear one, through a copper pommel, everything that consists of copper is known, modification being merely a clinging to words, only a name, it is only copper in reality.

5. 'Just as, O dear one, through a nail-parer, everything that consists of iron is known, modification being merely a clinging to words, only a name, it is only iron in reality - thus, my dear, is this instruction.'

6. 'Certainly my venerable teachers must not have known this teaching; because if they had known it, why would they not have communicated it to me? But venerable Sir, you will now please explain it to me!'

'So be it, my dear!

Chhandogya Upanishad, Sixth Chapter, First Part

*This passage is taken from the translation by V.M. Bedekar and G.B. Palsule

1. 'When, O dear one, the bees prepare honey, they gather the juice of manifold trees and assemble the juice into a unity.

2. 'So also, in that juice of these, no distinction is preserved as that of a particular tree whose juices they are; so also, indeed, O dear one, all these creatures, when they enter into the Being (in deep sleep and death), have no consciousness thereof, that they enter into the Being.

3. 'Whatever they may be here—a tiger, a lion or a wolf, or a bear, or a worm or a bird or a gadfly or a gnat, they are again born in these forms.

4. 'This universe consists of what that finest essence is, it is the real, it is the soul, that thou art, Svetaketu!'

5. 'Venerable Sir, teach me still further,' he (Svetaketu) said. 'So be it,' (Aruni) replied.

Chhandogya Upanishad, Sixth Chapter, Ninth Part

1. 'When one, O dear one, cuts this big tree here at the root, it trickles sap, because it lives; when one cuts it in the middle, it trickles sap, because it lives; when one cuts it at the top, it trickles sap, because it lives; thus it stands, penetrated through by the living self, prolific and rejoicing.

2. 'Now if life departs from one branch, that branch withers; if life departs from the second branch, that also withers; if life departs from the third branch, that also withers; if life departs from the whole tree, the whole tree withers or dries up. Therefore, O dear one, you should mark this he (Aruni) said.

3. 'This body indeed dies if it is deserted by life; but this life does not die. This universe consists of what that finest essence is; it is the real, it is the soul, that thou art, O Svetaketu.'

'Venerable Sir, teach me still further,' he (Svetaketu) said.

'So be it,' he (Aruni) replied.

Chhandogya Upanishad, Sixth Chapter, Eleventh Part

1. 'Fetch me a fruit of that Nyagrodha (banyan) tree there.'

'Here it is, venerable Sir,'
'Split it.'
'It is split, venerable Sir.'
'What do you see therein?'
'I see here, venerable Sir, very fine seeds.'
'Split one of them.'
'It is split, venerable Sir!'
'What do you see therein?'
'Nothing at all, venerable Sir!'

2. Then he (Aruni) spoke: 'That finest essence which you do not perceive, O dear one—out of this finest essence, indeed, this great Nyagrodha tree has arisen.

3. 'Believe, my dear, the universe consists of what that finest essence is; it is the real, it is the soul, that thou art, O Svetaketu!' 'Teach me still further, venerable Sir,' 'So be it,' he (Aruni) said.'

Chhandogya Upanishad, Sixth Chapter, Twelfth Part

1. 'Put this piece of salt, here, in water and come again tomorrow to me.' He did it. Then he (Aruni) said: 'Bring me the salt which you had put into the water last evening.' He groped, feeling after it and found nothing of it, because it was completely dissolved.

2. 'Taste that water from this side! How does it taste?'
'Saltish.'
'Taste it from the middle! How does it taste?'
'Saltish.'
Taste it from that side! How does it taste?'
'Saltish.'
'Let it be there; seat yourself by my side.'
He did it and said: 'It (salt in water) is always present.' Then the other one (Aruni said): 'Indeed, you do not perceive the Being here in the body but it is , nevertheless, therein.'

3. 'This universe consists of what that finest essence is, it is the real, it is the soul, that thou art, O Svetaketu!' 'Venerable Sir, instruct me still further!' 'So be it,' he (Aruni) said.

Chhandogya Upanishad, Sixth Chapter, Thirteenth Part

1. 'Just as, O dear one, a man who, with eyes bandaged, is led away out of the region of Gandhara and then forsaken in a deserted place, will grope breathlessly towards the north or towards the south, because he has been led away with bandaged eyes and has been left in an uninhabited place.

2. 'But thereafter somebody had removed the bandage from him and said to him: 'there lie the Gandhara regions beyond; go thither from here.' He reaches home in the Gandhara region, inquiring further from village to village, instructed by others and now quite sensible; in the same way man, who has here found a teacher, attains knowledge: 'I would belong to this drift of worldly existence until I have been released; thereafter I shall reach my home.'

3. 'This universe consists of what that finest essence is; it is the real, it is the soul, that thou art, O Svetaketu!'

Chhandogya Upanishad, Sixth Chapter, Fourteenth Part

IV*

Learning and the Knowledge of the Self

1. 'Teach me, venerable Sir!' With these words Narada approached Sanatkumara. He (Sanatkumara) said to him: 'Tell me what you already know; then I will impart to you what lies outside it.'

2. And the other (Narada) said, 'I have, O venerable Sir, learnt the Rigveda, Yajurveda, Samaveda, the Atharvaveda as the fourth, the epic and mythological poems as the fifth Veda, grammar, the ritual concerning the Manes, arithmetic, mantik, counting or reckoning of time, dialectic, politics, divine lore, the lore of the prayer, the lore of the ghosts, the science of warfare, astronomy, spell against serpents, the art of the muse [literally, of demigods, deva-jana]. This it is, O venerable Sir, that I have learnt.

3. 'And thus I am, O venerable Sir, no doubt learned in scriptures but not in the lore of the Atman. Because I have heard from such as are like you that he who knows the Atman, overcomes sorrow; but venerable Sir, I am afflicted with sorrow; that is why you will carry me, O Sir, to that yonder beach beyond sorrow!' And he (Sanatkumara) said to him: 'Everything that you have studied is mere name (naman).

4. 'The Rigveda, Yajurveda, Samaveda, the Atharvaveda as the fourth, the epic and mythological poems as the fifth Veda, grammar, the ritual of the Manes, arithmetic, mantik, reckoning of time, dialectic, politics, the divine lore, the lore of prayer, the lore of the ghosts, the science of warfare, astronomy, spell against serpents and the art of the muse—all these are a name, - everything of this is a name. You may adore the name!

5. 'He who adores the name as Brahman-so far as the name extends itself that far, over that extent, he will be entitled to move about according to his liking, that is why he adores the name as Brahman.' 'Is there, O venerable Sir, anything greater than the name?' 'Well there is one greater than the name.'

Chhandogya Upanishad, Seventh Chapter, First Part

*This passage is taken from the translation by V.M. Bedekar and G.B. Palsule.

Appendix II

Important Landmarks of Indian History

(Relevant to Indian Spirituality, Religion and Philosophy)

The ancient dates of Indian history are quite uncertain. The earliest records of Indian history are the Vedas, but the period, when they were composed, has been a matter of controversy and speculation. The Vedas themselves speak of the 'forefathers' who had achieved great spiritual conquests. The Vedas thus refer to a pre-Vedic period, during which, it is certain, the ancient forefathers of the Indian peoples had explored the secrets of the universe and produced momentous results.

Some historians have felt that the forefathers of Vedic sages must have lived around 10,000 B.C or even earlier. Some historians have tried to fix the dates of the Vedas on some basis of certain astronomical indications recorded in the Vedas, and they have concluded that the Vedas must have been composed around 4,500 B.C. Some conservative historians have, however, believed that the Vedas were composed around 2,000 B.C

It is thus clear that the first period of the ancient history of India cannot be accurately dated, but it is supposed to have been extended from an uncertain date upto the birth of Buddha. It is true that even the date of the birth of Buddha is somewhat controversial, but still, it was not later than 550 or 560 B.C

Thus the first period of the ancient Indian History may be said to extend from about 10,000 B.C (?) to 560 B.C

This period is generally called the Vedic period. Modern scholars divide it into three sub-periods: (1) the age of the Mantras (inevitable expressions of spiritual knowledge and power); (2) the age of the Brahmanas (prose writings in justification of Vedic rituals and practices); and (3) the age of the Upanishads (prose and poetical writings containing intuitions of spiritual explorers).

The Vedic age is also called the age of Intuition, and it is a source of the continuous stream of various spiritual, religious, philosophical and scientific movements that took place in the succeeding periods of Indian history.

The second period begins with the birth of the Buddha to the fall of the Mauryan empire. This covers the period from 560 B.C. to 200 B.C.

This period witnesses the remarkable life and work of the Buddha, the invasion of Alexander the great, the establishment of the Mauryan empire under the lead of Chandragupta Maurya and his adviser, Kautilya (or Chanakya), the life and work of Ashoka, who provided royal sanction to Buddhism and gave a great impetus to the spread of Buddhism not only in India but even in other Asian countries, and, finally, the decline and fall of the Mauryan empire. This period marks also the beginning of the Purano-Tantric age.

Psychologically, this period marks the transition from the age of Intuition to the age of Reason. The great epic literature (mainly the Ramayana and Mahabharta), great philosophical systems, codes of ethics, codes of statecraft as also great sciences and arts began to develop during this period. The great Purano-Tantric age, which began during this period, extends upto about 800 A.D

From 200 B.C to 300 A.D. India had a period of political uncertainty, and this came to an end with the rise of the Gupta empire beginning from 300 A.D. The Gupta period has been hailed in Indian history as a period of prosperity, opulence, richness, splendor and glory. The last great emperor of the Gupta period was Harsha. After him, the Gupta empire broke down around 700 A.D.

This marks the close of the ancient period in the history of India.

With the 8th century A.D. begins the medieval period of Indian history. The period extends upto the early 19th century. It is subdivided into the following sub-periods: (1) from 700 A.D. to 1200 A.D., extending from the fall of the Harsha's empire to the establishment of a Muslim kingdom in Delhi; (2) from 1200 to 1560 A.D., which extends from the establishment of the Muslim kingdom in Delhi to the rise of the Moghul empire of Akbar; and (3) from 1560 A.D. to 1800 A.D., extending from the early Moghul empire to the establishment of the British supremacy in India.

During this medieval period, there was a development of

intellectual philosophies such as those of Acharyas, notably, Shankara, Ramanuja, Madhwa and Vallabha. This was also a period of the spread of Shaivism and Vaishnavism. But more significantly, this was the age of a large number of Saints. This period is, therefore, also known as the age of Bhakti (Devotion). The greatest among the Saints who belonged to this period was Chaitanya (1485-1533).

During this period, there was also a great problem of receiving Islam, and two great attempts were made to arrive at a new synthesis; one from the side of the Muslims, and the other from the side of the Hindus. The former was exemplified in the attempt of Akbar (1542-1605) to create a new religion called Din-i-Ilahi, and the latter was exemplified by the life and work of Guru Nanak (1469-1538). The work of Guru Nanak gave rise to the subsequent Sikh Khalsa movement which was astonishingly original and novel.

During this period, there was a tremendous churning of the spirit of India, and a great attempt was made to explore all aspects of human being and to develop them in such a way that they could all open up to the spiritual light and force. This attempt had not only an individual aspect but also a collective aspect, and this was a remarkable attempt which could have revolutionized the collective life of India. But this was interrupted on account of several factors.

Among these factors was the fact of the exhaustion of the vital force as a result of a long march of effort from the earliest times of Indian history. This also coincided with the political instability and the coming of the settlers from the west, the French, the Dutch and the British. Finally, the political instability led to the establishment of the British supremacy in India.

In fact, the period following the death of Moghul emperor Aurangzeb (1707) marks a period of complete decline of Indian culture; and the Indian spirit was so much endangered during this period that even today India suffers from a tremendous inertia and obscurity.

Even then, the Indian spirit began to re-assert itself from the middle of the 19th century which marks the beginning of what has come to be called the Indian Renaissance.

The period, beginning from 1800 A.D., when the British established the supremacy in India, is generally called the modern period of Indian history. It was at the beginning of this period that there arose a galaxy of great personalities like Raja Rammohun Roy and Dayananda Saraswati, Sri Ramakrishna and Swami Vivekananda, who filled India with a new breath and sowed the seeds not only of a new spiritual awakening but also of social and political awakening. The great Indian fighters of India's freedom who struggled against the British were not only men and women of high spiritual attainments, but also of immense social and political dynamism. The new nationalist spirit was at once spiritual and social in character, and the great mantra of Indian nationalism (Vande Mataram: I bow to the Mother) symbolised a new vibration of spiritual and political force, which generated waves of nationalist movement and led India to her freedom on 15th August, 1947.

It is, however, important to note that the meaning and significance of the vast effort of Indian spirituality and culture began to be understood only in the context of what is happening since the turn of the century in the inner life of India. It is, in fact, through the life and work of Sri Aurobindo that India has taken not only a new course of an integral endeavor, but also in doing so, it has embraced quintessence of the vast Indian movement of the past and infused it with a new spirit and motivation, and while fulfilling the promises of the early effort, it has broken a new ground for the fulfillment not only of the Indian spirit but of the deepest aspirations of mankind.

It is this new movement which makes India so relevant to the modern world. It is that which makes the story of Indian culture so significant and meaningful. It is that which invites the attention of the world. It is that which is in the making and gives a call for a new light that can guide the human race in its further evolution.

This new story has begun, as noted above, from the turn of the twentieth century, and it is still in the process of shaping the contemporary moment and the coming Future.

Appendix III

A Note on the Vedic Literature

I

The antiquity of the Veda has been a subject of discussion and dispute. According to the ancient Indian tradition it is impossible to determine the period of the composition of the Veda. It is, however, universally acknowledged by historians that the Veda is the earliest available collection of the most ancient body of knowledge. According to one of the Indian historians, Shri Avinash Chandra Das, Vedas could have been composed any time between 250th and 750th century B.C. According to Lokamanya Tilak, the estimated period would be any time between 45th and 50th century B.C. This coincides with the view of Professor Haug, Professor Ludwig and Professor Jacobi. Professor Whitney places this period any time between 15th and 20th century B.C., while Professor Weber places it any time between 12th and 15th century B.C. Professor Max Muller believes that the Veda was composed during the 13th century B.C.

According to Brihadāranyakopanishad, all the four Vedas, Rigveda, Yajurveda, Sāmaveda and Atharvaveda, are the breath of the Supreme Lord.

> अस्य महतो भूतस्य निःश्वसितम् एतद् यद् ऋग्वेदो
> यजुर्वेदः सामवेदोऽथर्वांगिरसः।

According to Manu Smriti, the entire Veda is luminous with knowledge (सर्वज्ञानमयो हि सः). It is believed that in its original condition Veda was one, but it was Rishi Vyāsa who divided it into four parts. For this reason, Rishi Vyāsa is known as Vedavyāsa. The four Vedas have been divided in many ways under the categories of *mandala, ashtaka, varga, sukta, anuvāk, khānda, prashna, chhanda,* etc. Every word of the poetic and prose composition of the Veda has been counted and fixed. The entire collection of the mantras is called "Samhitā". According to one view, the word Veda is applicable to both the collection of the mantras (inevitable expressions of poetic inspiration and revelation) and Brāhmanas. Brāhmanas are supposed to be detailed analysis and commentary on the collection of the mantras. Brāhmanas again are divided into three parts, (i) Brāhmanas, (ii) Āranyakas and (iii) Upanishads. In the Brāhmanas, there is a detailed statement and explanation of various kinds of sacrifices and their ceremonies and rituals. Āranyakas are much more esoteric and Upanishads expound the knowledge contained in the Vedas. Upanishads are also called *vedānta.* At a later period, Rishi Bādarāyana Vyāsa composed Brahmasūtra or Sariraksutra in order to present the Upanishads in an organised form. At a still later period, *Bhagvad Gita* was composed as a part of the great *Mahābhārata* and it is considered to be the quint-essence of the Upanishads. The *Upanishad, Brahmasutra and Bhagavad Gitā* are collectively *Prasthānatrayi.*

The Vedic literature mainly consists of mantra samhitā, Brāhmanas, Āranyakas and Upanishads. In understanding the mantra samhita, the study of Brāhmanas, Āranyakas and Upanishads is considered to be essential, and the study of Brahmasutra and *Bhagvad Gita* is also considered to be necessary. Vedic literature also includes six additional works which are supposed to be aids in understanding the Veda. They are: (i) Shikshā, (ii) Kalpa, (iii) Vyākarana, (iv) Nirukta, (v) Chhanda and (vi) Jyotisha. Each one of them is called Vedānga.

Connected with the rituals and ceremonies of Vedic sacrifices (Vedic Karmakānda), is the Vedānga known as Kalpa. Kalpa Vedanga is in the form of sūtra, and it is thus aphoristic in character. The totality of the Kalpa Vedānga and its literature is threefold, consisting of Shrauta Sūtra, Grihya Sūtra and Dharma Sūtra. For each Veda there are separate systems of Shrauta Sūtra, Grihya Sūtra and Dharma Sūtra. Some of the famous Shrauta Sūtras are Shānkhāyana, Āshvalāyan, Ārsheya, Āpastamba, Baudhāyana, and Kātyāyana. Among the Grihya Sūtras are included Shānkhyāna, Hiranyakeshi, Āpastamba, Baudhāyana, Kāthaka, Pārāskāra, Kaushika, etc. Among the Dharma Sūtras are included Gautama Dharma Sūtra, Āpastamba Dharma Sūtra, Hiranykeshi Dharma Sūtra, Baudhāyana Dharma Sūtra, Vasishtha Dharma Sūtra.

In addition to these three categories of Kalpa Sūtras, there is a fourth category known as Shulba Sūtra which is regarded to be the origin of the ancient science of geometry. Three most famous Shulba Sutras are those of Āpastamba, Baudhāyana and Kātyāyana. As in the case of Kalpa Vedānga, each of the Vedangas has further subsidiary literature. All this and much more may be regarded to constitute the vast Vedic literature. Itihāsa, Purānas and Vedic systems of philosophy also are included as parts of the Vedic literature.

II

But as mentioned above, the core of the Vedic literature consists, mainly of Mantra Samhitā, Brāhmanas, Āranyakas and Upanishads.

Among the Vedas, Rigveda occupies a prominent place. Rigveda consists of 10 Books or Mandalas and 1017 hymns or Sūktas. Total number of Verses in Rigveda is 10,580. Even the words and letters of the Rigveda have been counted. The number of words in the Rigveda is 1,53,826 and the number of letters is 4,32,000. Some of the great names of the poets who have received the mantras include Vasishtha, Vishwāmitra, Vāmadeva, Bhāradwāja, Atri, Madhuchhandas. Six of the Mandalas or books are given each to the hymns of a single Rishi or family of Rishis. Thus the second Mandala is devoted chiefly to the sūktas of the Rishi Gritsamada, the third and the seventh similarly to the great names of Vishwāmitra and Vasishtha, respectively, the fourth to Vāmadeva, the sixth to Bhāradwāja. The fifth is occupied by the hymns of the house of Atri. In each of these Mandalas the sūtras addressed to Agni are first collected together, followed by those of which Indra is the deity; the invocations of other Gods, Brihaspati, Sūrya, the Ribhus, Ushā, etc., close the Mandalas. The whole book, the ninth, is given to a single God, Soma. The first, eighth and tenth Mandalas are collections of Sūtras by various Rishis, but the hymns of each seer are ordinarily placed together in the order of their deities, Agni leading, Indra following, the other Gods succeeding.

We can also see a certain principle of thought development in the arrangement of the Vedic hymns. The opening Mandala seems to have been so designed that the general thought of the Veda in its various elements should correctly unroll itself under the cover of the established symbols by the voices of a certain number of Rishis who almost all rank high as thinkers and sacred singers and are, some of them, among the most famous names of Vedic tradition. It is also significant that the tenth or closing Mandala gives us, with an even greater miscellaneity of authors, the last development of the thought of the Veda, and some of the most modern in language of its sūtras. It is here that we find the Sacrifice of Purusha and the great Hymn of the Creation. It is here also that modern scholars think that they discover the first origins of the Vedāntic philosophy, the Brahmavāda.

Sacrifice was the principal institution and symbol of the Vedic tradition and knowledge. Sacrifice or yajna symbolises inner submission, consecration and surrender to higher powers, gods and the Supreme. Outwardly, this submission was translated into an elaborate ritual of collecting sacrificial materials, lighting them in order to kindle the sacrificial fire and offering to that fire articles of various kinds, including clarified butter, grains, and other materials. This entire procedure was accompanied by recitation of appropriate mantras or hymns, sung in the prescribed methodical manner, often marked by appropriate hand movements and other gestures or mudrās. The esoteric teaching of the Veda included the idea that human life is a journey, looked upon as a journey of sacrifice to be performed with minute care and attention to discipline and self-control by means of which obstacles in the journey can be overcome and many-sided achievements at various levels of existence can be attained. A close connection was conceived between the word, the idea and the reality, and it was supposed that words opened up the gates of ideas and ideas opened up the gates of the realisation of reality. It was against this background that the ritual of yajna was perfected in great detail, and apart from the worship, great attention was paid to the performance of sacrifice. The priest who performed the entire procedure of the sacrifice was called Adhvaryu, and the mantras which were used by the Adhvaryu in the performance of yajna constituted Yajurveda. Yajurveda is therefore also called Adhvaryuveda. Yajurveda is principally a composition in prose.

According to *Matsyapurāna*, Yajurveda was the only Veda in the beginning. The same view is repeated in *Vayupurāna* and *Vishnupurāna*. It was Vedavyāsa who arranged four Samhitās according to the requirements of the processes of symbolic sacrifice, and he transmitted Rigveda to Paila, Yajurveda to Vaishampāyana, Sāmaveda to Jaimini, and Atharvaveda to Sumantu. In due course, they transmitted them to their pupils, and thereafter there developed the tradition of transmission by oral tradition from teacher to pupil, and in this fashion, there came about a development of various recensions or Shākhās of various Vedas. In Bhāgavata and in several Purānas there is a detailed description of various Shākhās of the Vedas; and we have also a similar description in *Shāntiparva* (Chapter 342) of *Mahābhārata;* we have also an organised information on the the Shākhās of the Vedas in *Charanavyūha*. There are three notable books of *Charanavyūha* attributed, respectively, to Shaunaka, Kātyāyana and Vyāsa.

The total number of Shākhās are believed to be 1131, but at present only 10 Shākhās remain alive. As far as Rigveda is concerned, only one Shākhā, Shākala Shākhā alone remains alive out of the 21 which existed at one time. There is a claim that Sañkhyāyana Shākhā is still known to a few Vedapāthis in Uttar Pradesh and Gujarat, but this is not certain. As far as Yajurveda is concerned, Patanjali had declared in his great *Vyākarana Mahābhāshya* that it had 101 Shākhās. But today only 5 Shākhās are alive. In fact, Yajurveda is classified broadly into Shukla Yajurveda and Krishna Yajurveda. Shukla Yajurveda is also known as Vājasaneyi. Vājasaneyi Samhitā has 30 Adhyāyas or Chapters, 303 Anuvaks, 1975 Kandikās, 29625 words, and 88875 letters. There are two extant Shākhās of Shukla or Vājasaneyi Yajurveda, namely, Kānwa and Mādhyandina. Krishna Yajurveda has 5 extant Shākhās, namely, Āpastamba (Taittiriya), Hiranyakeshi (Kapishthala)*, Katha*, Kāthaka, and Kālāpa or Maitrāyanī. Maitrāyanī Samhitā has 4 Kāndas which are sub-divided into Prapāthakas. In this Samhitā, there are 3144 mantras, of which 1701 are Riks from Rigveda. In this Samhita we have mantras and rituals of the important sacrifices like those of Chāturmāsya, Vājapeya, Ashwamedha, Rājasūya, Sautrāmani, etc. Taittiriya Samhitā has 7 Kāndas, 44 Prapāthakas and 631 Anuvaks. In this Samhitā we have the description of sacrifices like Rājasūya, Yajamāna, Paurodāsha, etc.

Apart from Adhvaryu, there is also Udgātā in a sacrifice, who sings certain specific mantras. The collection of mantras meant for Udgātā has been called Sāmaveda. Both in *Charanavyūha* and in *Patanjali Mahābhāshya* it is indicated that Sāmaveda had 1000 Shākhās. Sāmaveda is musical in character, and it contains only those Riks which can appropriately be sung. There are 1549 Riks in Sāmaveda, and only 75 of them are independent of Rigveda. At present, Sāmaveda has only 3 existing Shākhās, namely Kauthuma, Rānāyaniya, and Jaiminiya.

The Riks are transformed into songs of Sāma by appropriate addition of words or stobhas, such as hā, u, ho, i, o, ho, oh, ou, hā, etc.

* Incomplete versions only are available

Apart from 'hotā' connected with Rigveda, 'Adhvaryu' connected with Yajurveda, 'Udgātā' connected with Sāmaveda, there is a fourth priest called Brahmā who is supposed to be a specialist of all the four Vedas, including Atharvaveda. Rigveda, Yajurveda and Sāmaveda are collectively called Vedatrayi, and Atharvaveda is not included in the Vedatrayi, although it has significant place in the Karmakānda of the Vedas. Atharvaveda is also known as Atharvāngirasa Atharvaveda has two kinds of mantras, those relating to the cure of diseases and destruction of wild animals, pishāchas and enemies, and those relating to establishment of peace in family and village as also those relating to health, wealth, protection, and friendship with enemies. The origin of Āyurveda is to be found in Atharvaveda.

The Samhitā of Atharvaveda has 20 Kāndas which have 34 prapāthakas, 111 Anuvaks, 739 Sūktas and 5849 mantras. About 1200 mantras are common with those of Rigveda. 1/6 part of the Atharvaveda is in the prose style while the rest is poetic.

Patanjali has indicated that Atharvaveda has 9 Shākhās, but today we have only 2 Shākhās, namely, Paippalāda and Shaunaka.

Apart from four Vedas and their numerous Shākhās, there is a vast literature of Brahmanas. The appendices of Brāhmanas which are partly in prose and partly in poetic form are called Āranyakas. Āranyakas are so called because there was a tradition to study them in forests. Some Upanishads are also included in Āranyakas; hence it is almost impossible to make a definite boundary-line between Āranyakas and Upanishads. Brāhmanas contain detailed analysis of various categories of sacrifices, their rituals and procedures. Brāhmanas include collections of history, legends, anecdotes and narration of stories connected with individuals. A synonym of the word "Brāhmanas" is "Pravachana". Pravachana means exposition; hence Brāhmanas are looked upon as expositions of various aspects of the Vedas. The Brāhmana literature seems to have been very vast, but a number of Brāhmanas have been lost.

Each of the recensions of the Vedas had a separate Brāhmana. Brāhmanas were instructed simultaneously with the different recensions of the Vedas. The Aitareya Brāhmana belongs to the Shākala Shākhā of Rigveda, while Kaushitaki (Shānkhāyana) Brāhmana is connected with Bashkala Shākhā of Rigveda. Shatapatha Brāhmana is connected with Shukla Yajurveda, while Taittiriya Brāhmana and Kāthaka Brāhmana are connected with Krishna

Yajurveda. Sāmaveda has several Brahmanas including Jaiminiya, Ārsheya, Mantra, Sāmavidhāna, Devatādhāya Vansha, Panchavinsha Shadavinsha. Gopatha Brāhmana belongs to Atharvaveda.

Among the lost Brahmanas, the important ones are Paimgāyani Brāhmana, Āshvalāyana Brāhmana, Gālav Brāhmana, Charak Brāhmana, Shwetāshvatara Brāhmana, Kāthava Brāhmana, Maitrayāni Brāhmana, Jhābālak Brāhmana, Khāndikeya Brāhmana, Rauraki Brāhmana, Shatyāyana Brāhmana, Talavakara Brāhmana, Āruneya Brāhmana, Pārāshara Brāhmana, and Kāpeya Brāhmana.

According to many ancient scholars hymns of the four Vedas and their explanations in the Brāhmanas both together constitute the Veda. The Brāhmanas have been throughout respected as the Veda itself. The rituals have been performed considering the Brāhmanas as equal to the Vedas. In the 19th century, however, Maharshi Dayananda Saraswati expressed the view that the Brāhmanas are not the Veda itself. According to him, while Vedas were revealed, Brāhmanas were not, although they were expressed by the seers. He advanced a number of reasons to establish his view-point, and they deserve an impartial study. In any case, it has to be stated that the language of the Brāhmana is not similar to that of the Vedic hymns. Some believe that Brāhmanas contain explanation of the Veda and they are couched in the language of Pravachana. They are therefore Vedic, but not the Veda itself. There is, however, no dispute about the fact that Brāhmanas are looked upon as elucidation or interpretations of Veda, and this itself implies the superiority of Veda as far as the question of authenticity is concerned.

There is no doubt that Brāhmanas were much more close in time to the Vedas than any other Vedic literature; at the same time, it is well known that Brāhmanas concentrated on Karmakānda rather than on Jnānakānda. As far as the Jnānakānda is concerned, we have a vast literature of Āranyakas and Upanishads. Āranyakas and Upanishads are collectively called Vedānta, since they constitute the last part of the fundamental core of the Vedic literature.

The main subject dealt with the Āranyakas is the esoteric meaning of sacrifices, their rituals as also the inner meaning of the conduct related to the system of *varnāshrama.* Aitareya and Kaushitaki Āranyakas are related to Rigveda, Taittiriya and Sānkhayāyana Āranyakas are related to Krishna Yajurveda, while

Brihadāranyaka is related to Shukla Yajurveda. Talavakara Āranyaka belongs to Jaiminiya Shākhā of Samaveda; and in fact this Āranyaka is Jaiminiya-Brāhmanopanishadbrāhmana, and this Brāhmana contains Āranyaka and Upanishad as well.

The most important Āranyaka is the Aitareya Āranyaka of Rigveda. This Āranyaka consists of 18 Chapters, and each Chapter is divided into a number of khandas. As mentioned earlier, Āranyakas deal with the inner meanings of various sacrifices, observances and rituals.

The spiritual meaning of the Veda is largely to be found in Upanishads. The word Upanishad really means the secret teaching that enters into the ultimate truth. This secret is normally transmitted and received when the disciple sits close to the teacher, and when the consciousness of the teacher and pupil vibrates in harmony, so that even in silence the secret truth can be transmitted and received. Among the Upanishads the following 10 are considered to be most important: Isha, Kena, Katha, Prashna, Mundaka, Māndukya, Taittiriya, Chhāndogya, Aitareya, and Brihadāranyaka. Shankarācharya has also referred to 5 other Upanishads in his Commentaries, and these 5 also have been given prominence as far as the spiritual knowledge of the ultimate reality is concerned. They are: Shwetāshvatara, Mahānārāyana, Maitrāyāni, Kaushitakī, and Nrisimhatāpinī.

In the *Muktopanishad*, it is mentioned that the total number of Upanishad is 108, and they are derived from the 4 Vedas as follows: (i) Rigveda: 10 Upanishads, (2) Shukla Yajurveda: 19 Upanishads, (3) Krishna Yajurveda: 32 Upanishads, (4) Samaveda: 16 Upanishads and (5) Atharvaveda: 31 Upanishads. *Muktopanishad* also lays down that the process of the realisation of the Brahman, the ultimate reality, begins with Brahmajijnāsa, aspiration to know the Brahman, and it continues through the hearing of the Upanishads, reflection on the Upanishads and dwelling on the Upanishads.

Isha, Kena, Katha Mundaka, Shwetāshvatara and Mahānārāyāna are poetic compositions and they have great literary merits. Atharvaveda has many Upanishads, and among these Upanishads there are some which are even non-Vedic, in the sense that they have connection with Purānas and Tantra. If the entire Upanishadic literature is taken into account, there are at least 250 Upanishads.

The important Upanishads and their connections with the Vedas may briefly be stated in the following table:

Aitareya, Māndukya and Kaushitaki are related to Rigveda;
Taittiriya, Katha, and Shwetāshvatara are connected with Krishna Yajurveda;
Brihadāranyaka and Isha are related to Shukla Yajurveda;
Kena and Chhāndogya are related to Sāmaveda; and
Prashna and Manduka are related to Atharvaveda.

In spite of the fact that the Upanishads are not as remote as the Veda in respect of language and symbolism, they are extremely difficult to understand. Upanishads should be looked upon as vehicles of illumination and not of instruction; they were composed for seekers who had already a general familiarity with the ideas of the Vedic and Vedāntic seers and even some personal experience of the truths on which they were founded. This is why they dispense in their style with expressed transitions of thought and the development of implied or subordinate notions. Very often one single word or sentence reposes on a number of ideas implicit in the text but nowhere set forth explicitly. The reasoning that supports conclusions is often suggested by words but not expressly conveyed to the intelligence. The reader, or rather the hearer, was supposed to proceed from light to light, confirming his intuition and verifying by his experience, not submitting the ideas to the judgements of the logical reason. As a result, Upanishads demand a good deal of patience, quietude and concentration, if we are to understand them properly. Even then it is difficult to penetrate into the inner meaning of the Upanishads.

There have been numerous commentators, and during the middle ages, there have been sharp differences of opinion even as to the fundamental principles of the philosophy of the Upanishads. This has given rise to at least 5 major schools of the Upanishadic interpretation. These are: Advaitavāda or Monism of Shankarācharya, Vishishtādvaita or Qualified Monism of Rāmānujāchārya, Vishuddhādvaitavada or Pure Monism of Vallabhāchārya, Dvaitādvaitavāda or Dualism-non-Dualism of Nimbārkāchārya, and Dvaitavāda or Dualism of Madhawachārya. The commentaries of these great Ācharyas are commentaries on *Brahmasutra* which was composed by Bādarāyana (Vyasa Rishi) in which the secret of the Upanishads was expounded aphoristically. The commentaries of the Ācharyas have been further commented upon by their disciples and there have been commentaries on commentaries. *Bhagavad Gita* is also considered to be an organised exposition of the essence of the Upanishadic teaching; but *Bhagavad Gita* also has been interpreted differently by different Ācharyas, and there have been a number of commentaries on the *Bhagavad Gita*. The commentary literature on the *Upanishads, Brahmasūtra,* and *Bhagavad Gita* is continuing to develop even in our own times.

III

Vedic literature includes in its comprehensive sense the Vedānga literature as well. Vedānga literature began to develop even before the Upanishads. Mundaka Upanishad mentions 6 Vedāngas as follows: (i) Shikshā, (ii) Kalpa, (iii) Vyākarana, (iv) Nirukta, (v) Chhanda, and (vi) Jyotisha. Each Vedānga takes up one aspect of the Veda and an attempt is made to explain it.

Shikshā is related to sound, letters, pronunciation, the method of teaching and learning of these basic elements. Every Veda has its own peculiar pronunciation of certain letters, and each one of them has its specific modes and speed of recitation. A book called *Shikshā Sangraha* contains a collection of 32 systems of Shikshā. These systems relate to different Shākhās of the 4 Vedas. The most important among the books relating to Shikshā is the famous *Pāniniya Shikshā*. Another important book is *Yājnavalkiya Shikshā*. In *Vasishthi Shikshā* we have a detailed account of the differences between the mantras of the Rigveda and Yajurveda. Both *Yājnavalkiya Shikshā* and *Vasishthi Shikshā* are related to the Vajasaneyi Samhitā. The other important works are: Katyāyani Shikshā, Pārāshari Shiksha, Mādhyandini Shiksha, Keshavi Shiksha and Manduki Shikshā. In the Nāradiya Shikshā, which is related to Sāmaveda, there is supposed to be the knowledge of the secret of different sounds.

The development of Shikshā as a Vedanga and as a science demonstrates profundity and vast scope of research that was undertaken in respect of pronunciation in ancient India. It is because of this Vedānga that the system of Vedic recitation has remained intact right from the ancient times to the present day. A given Shākhā is recited in the same way all over the country, and

Vedapāthis of the same Shākhā, belonging to different parts of India, pronounce mantras with the same intonation, speed and strength and force, and even the same gestures of hand movements. If the Vedānga system of pronunciation has remained so uniform in the country and if the tradition has remained so powerful, it is because of the degree of perfection that was achieved in respect of Shikshā.

The Vedic religion involves complex ritualistic Karmakānda (system of prescribed acts and sacrifices). A detailed understanding of this Karmakānda became necessary in due course of time, and this gave rise to a vast literature of Kalpasūtra. Kalpa means that which is understood or justified in respect of sacrifices and other prescribed acts and rituals. Karmakānda is three-fold : Shrautasūtras, which are connected with sacrifices laid down in Shruti or Veda; Grihyasūtras, which are related to various rituals connected with the life of the householder, and various Samskāras which are laid down for important occasions of life starting from birth upto death; and Dharmasūtras which are related to social, political and other benevolent duties. The entire Kalpa literature is Sūtra literature, since it is composed aphoristically. There is also a fourth category of Kalpa Sūtra, which is known as Shulbasūtra, and which is related to the science of geometry and architecture connected with the construction of sacrificial altars, fire-vessels and other related structures.

Corresponding to each Veda there are various Shrauta Sūtras. Shānkhyāyana and Āshwalāyana pertain to Rigveda; Ārsheya (or Māshaka), Lāhyāyana and Drāhyāyana belong to Sāmaveda; Āpastamba, Hiranyakeshi, Baudhāyana, Bhārdwaja, and Vaikhānasa are related to the Taittiriya Shākhā of Krishna Yajurveda; Mānava Shrauta Sūtra is related to Maitrayāni Shākhā of Krishna Yajur Veda (this Sūtra is believed to be the basis of the famous Manu Samriti); Kātyāyana Shrauta Sūtra is related to Shukla Yajurveda; Vaitāna Sūtra is related to Atharvaveda, and this Sutra is also related to Gopatha Brāhmana and Kātyāyana Shrauta Sutra of Yajurveda.

The sacrificial priest needs to have appropriate knowledge of all the Shrauta Sūtras connected with the four Vedas. In some of the sacrifices, as many as 16 priests are required. There are 14 kinds of sacrificial acts, of which 7 are Havir Yajna and 7 are Soma Yajna. Of the Havir Yajna the important sacrifices are those of

Darshapoornamāsya and Chaturmāsya. In Soma Yajna the important ritual is that of Agnishtoma. Soma Yajnas are of the three kinds, those which are for one day (ekāha), those of 12 days (dwādashāha), and those of many days (anekāha). Agnichayana connected with Soma Yajna continues for one complete year.

Grihya Sūtras, which come after Shrauta Sūtras, also belong to different Vedas. Shānkhāyāyana Grihya Sūtra, Shāmbavya Grihya Sūtra, and Āshwalāyana Grihya Sūtra are related to Rigveda; Gomila and Khādira belong to Sāmaveda; Āpastamba, Hiranyakeshi, Baudhāyana, Mānava, Kāthaka, Bhāradwāja and Vaikhānasa belong to Krishna Yajurveda, while Pāraskara belongs to Shukla Yajurveda; Kaushika Grihya Sutra belongs to Atharvaveda.

The various rituals described in Shrauta Sūtra require three different kinds of Agnikundas (fire - vessels) which are called Garhāpatya, Āhavaniya and Dakshina, while in the Deva Yajna prescribed by Grihya Sūtra only one Agnikunda is required.

Among the Dharma Sūtras, Gautama Dharma Sūtra is related to Sāmaveda, and Āpastamba, Hiranyakeshi, and Baudhāyana are related to Krishna Yajurveda. But Dharma Sūtras such as Gautama, Vasishtha, Mānava, Vaikhānasa and Vishnu are not related to any specific Veda Shākhā.

The word *"dharma"* has been used in various senses in Indian literature. According to Manu Smriti, *dharma* is characterised by what is contained in the Veda, in the Smriti, and in what is involved in the conduct of good and noble people as also what is good for the one's inner soul. In Sanskrit literature, the word "Dharma Shāstra" is largely connected with all the Smritis beginning with Manu and Yājnavalkya and which is in conformity with the Vedas. The Dharma literature begins with the Dharma Sūtra of Gautama, Baudhāyana and Āpastamba which appear to belong to 7th to 4th century B.C. In due course, the Dharma literature flourished extensively and as many as 100 Smritis seem to have been composed; some of them are in prose, but many are in poetic form. Among the authors of Smritis, Manu is the foremost, and there have been a large number of commentaries on Manu Smriti. Among these commentaries, the prominent ones are those of Medhātithi, Govindarāja, Kullukabhatta, Nārāyana, Rāghavānanda, Nandana and Rāmachandra.

The subject of Dharma has also been dealt with in some detail in the *Bhagavad Gita,* which is the greatest gospel of Karmayoga and in which we find the greatest ancient synthesis of Karma, Jnāna and Bhakti. The *Bhagavad Gita* recognises an evolutionary system of Dharma, by means of which the individual and the society can be helped in their evolutionary and progressive development towards perfection. In the course of this development, there are also important concepts of svadharma and svakarma. And in the culminating chapter of the *Gita*, we find Lord Krishna asking Arjuna to renounce all Dharmas and to surrender to the Supreme Divine.

This vast and complex teaching of the *Gita* seems to be inherent in the teaching of the Veda, which is also the original synthesis of Karma, Jnāna and Bhakti. The master concept of the Veda from which the concept of Dharma developed in the later period is that of Ritam. Ritam and Satyam seem to be interchangeable, but there is a certain distinction between the two in so far as Satyam may be regarded to be the *truth* and Ritam to be the *right*. In fact, the full formula of perfection as defined in the Veda is Satyam, Ritam, and Brihat. Brihat or the vast is the fundamental perspective of the truth. Where there is limitation, there is partiality and there is imperfection or distortion of truth. It is only in the context of the vast infinitude that truth can be apprehended, comprehended and known, and it is only when truth is known that right action can proceed. This is the significance of the trinity of satyam, ritam and brihat.

If we keep firm on this original meaning of ritam, we can appreciate the entire development of the concept of Dharma in Indian literature. Dharma is that which holds us, which gives us cohesion, and which keeps us fixed on the progressive path of development and growth. In this context, there can not be static Dharma, and there can not be one uniform Dharma for all human beings and for all levels of life. What is right for a tāmasika (dull) being cannot be right for the rājasika (passionate or dynamic), and what is right for the rājasika cannot be right for the sāttwika (pure and luminous). And since sāttwika is still not the highest, what is right for the sāttwika cannot be binding on the one who transcends even the golden fetters of the sattwa. The one who transcends the chain of tamas, rajas and sattwa and enters into the infinitude, the Brihat of the Veda, he becomes capable of transcending all dharmas which are appropriate to lower developments through tamas, rajas and sattwa. He is liberated from the egoistic limitations, he becomes capable of total surrender to the

Supreme, and in a state of comprehension of the truth, satyam, he becomes capable of the right action, ritam.

It is against this background of the concept of ritam and dharma that we can better appreciate the entire history of the Dharmashāstra in India, where there has been strict insistence on adherence to social law and yet complex and flexible application of it, and even a supervening tendency to preach transcendence of all good and evil and all the binding chains of dharma.

We come next to Nirukta. Nirukta is a kind of commentary on Nighantu which is a collection of difficult words of the Veda. Nighantu is supposed to have been composed by Prajāpati Kashyap. In the first two chapters, Nighantu provides a collection of those words which have one meaning, and in the fourth chapter, it gives a collection of those words which have several meanings. In the fifth chapter, the names of Vedic gods have been collected. There have been many commentaries on Nighantu, but it is the commentaries on Nighantu, but it is the commentary of Yāska, which has found its place as one of the Vedāngas, and this Vedanga is known as Nirukta. Nirukta is not confined only to meanings of words; it traces the words to their originals, and it indicates how different similar or dissimilar words arose from those origins. The principle that all names are originated from verbs is an important principle of Nirukta, and even modern linguists accept this principle. It is believed that Yāska lived some time between 10th and 8th century B.C. Prior to Yāska also, there were many methods and systems of Vedic interpretation, such as Ādhi-daivata, Ādhyātma, Ākhyāna-Samaya, Aithihāsika, Naidāna, Pārivrājaka, Yājnika, etc. By the time we come to Yāska, the original meanings of many words had become obscure, and he mentions several words where there is no certainty of their meanings.

According to a belief propounded by Kautsa, Vedas have no meaning. Yāska opposed this belief and he said:

"स्थानुरयं भारहरः किलाभूत्। अधीत्य वेदान् न विजानाति यो ऽ थर्म्।
यो ऽ र्थज्ञ इत् सकलं भद्रमश्नुते। नाकमेति ज्ञानविधूतपाप्मा॥"

He has thus compared him, who does not know the meaning of the Veda, to an inert bearer of Veda. According to him, one who attains to the knowledge of meaning becomes free from sin and proceeds towards heaven.

There have been several commentaries on Nirukta such as those of Durgāchārya, Skanda Maheshwara and Vararuchi.

Nirukta deals with various subjects which are very close to Grammar or Vyākarana, and therefore Nirukta is often considered to be a part of Vyākarna. However, Vyākarana is considered to be a principal part of the six Vedāngas.Vyākarana is looked upon as the mouth among the Vedāngas. According to the ancient tradition, Brahmā was the first to expound Vyākarana, and he was followed by Grammarians like Brihaspati, Indra, Maheshwara, etc. The most celebrated author of Vyākarana is Pānini, who has himself mentioned several great names of the great Grammarians. Pānini's famous book is *Ashtādhyāyi*, in which he has discussed both Vedic and non-Vedic words. There have been numerous Grammarians who followed Pānini between 1st century B.C. upto 14th century A.D. Some believe that Pānini belonged to 7th century B.C., while others place him in the 4th century A.D. According to Yuddhishthira Mimānsaka, Pānini belonged to 2900 years before the beginning of Vikram Era, which is supposed to be 200 years after the Mahābhārata war.

One of the greatest commentaries on Vyākarana is that of Patanjali. This is supposed to be the most authentic book on Pānini's Vyākarana. The authenticity of Patanjali's commentary is so great that wherever there is a difference of opinion between *Sūtra, Vārttika and Mahābhāshya,* the verdict of *Mahābhāshya* of Patanjali is regarded to be ultimately acceptable. According to Western scholars, Patanjali belonged to 2nd century B.C. According to Yuddhishthira Mimānsaka, Patanjali belonged to 2000 or 1200 years before the Vikram Era.

In the 16th century A.D., the method of the study of Grammar propounded by Pānini began to be replaced to some extent by tradition of Kātantra. In that tradition, *Siddhānta Kaumudi* of Bhattoji Dikshit and *Prakriyā Sarvasa* of Nārayāna Bhatta are more prominent. Vyākarana developed also in the field of philosophy, and this was initiated by Bhratrihari who belonged to the 6th century A.D.

The composition of the Vedas indicates consummate development of the knowledge of the poetic meter, *Chhandas.* The first discussion on Vedic meters is to be found in the Sānkhyāyana Shrauta Sūtra. But the classical work on meters is that of Maharshi Pingal. Meters or Chhandas have been studied by Pingal in the eighth Chapter of his book *Chhandah Sūtra*. In this book, he has taken into account not only Vedic meters but also others. There are mainly 7 Vedic meters, namely, Gayatrī, Ushnik, Anushtubh, Brihatī, Pankti, Trishtubh, and Jagatī. According to Kātyāyana, the highest number of mantras in Rigveda are to be found in Trishtubh. This number is 4253. Gāyatrī has 2467 mantras; Jagatī has 1350 mantras; Anushtubh has 855 mantras; Ushnik has 341 mantras; Pankti has 312 mantras, and Brihatī has 181 mantras. Although there are numerous meters, we find only 50 meters in the Sanskrit literature.

Prior to Pingalāchārya, there were several great teachers of Chhanda Shastra, such as Koshtuki, Yāska, Kāshyapa, and Māndavya. There have been several commentaries on the Chhanda Sūtra of Pingalācharya. In fact, there has been a continuous development of books on Chhanda Shāstra in the Sanskrit literature.

The development of musical science also owes a great deal to Chhanda Shāstra. It is well known that Sāmaveda is meant to be sung. Although the method of singing Sāma is different from that of the classical music, the 7 tunes, namely, shadja, rishabha, gāndhara, madhyama, panchama, dhaivata, and nishāda are used in Sāma in the same way as in the classical music. In the *Chhāndogyopanishad* which is based upon Samaveda, 5 types of the musical renderings of Sāma have been indicated, namely, Himkāra, Prastāva, Udgitha, Pratihār, and Nidhān. It is noteworthy that Vedic literature refers also to several musical instruments, including the Veena. In the social life, too, because of the close connection between religious rites and music, various melodies developed, particularly 6 melodies corresponding to 6 seasons. Closely connected with music waṣ the development of dance and drama. Among the important works in Sanskrit regarding music, dance, and drama the most important one is Natya Shastra of Bharat Muni. There are two Samhitās on Nātya Shāstra, namely, dwādasha sahasri and shat sahasri. The traditions established by Bharat Muni remained prevalent for more than thousand years, and even in the book *Sangeet Ratnākar* of Sharangadeva of 13th century A.D., the authority of Bharat Muni has been acknowledged. Thereafter also there has been a vast literature on music, dance, and drama. In fact, music, dance, and drama received royal patronage throughout the ages, and even some of the great kings of the North and the South were themselves great musicians.

Closely connected with Shikshā, Chhanda and Vyākarana, there is a body of literature known as Prātishākhya. For each Veda and for each Shākhā there are certain specific rules, and these rules deal with various subjects connected with pronunciation, meters, and various grammatical matters. The meaning of the Veda is also indicated in the Prātishākhya, and it is therefore considered to be an aid to the study of the concerned Veda. The Rik Prātishākhya deals with Shaishiriya Upashākhā of the Shākala Shākhā of the Rigveda. Maharshi Shaunaka is the author. The great commentator Uvat has written a commentary on this Prātishākhya. It is believed that Rik Prātishākhya was composed between 5th and 6th century, A.D.

Vajasaneyi Prātishākhya was composed by Kātyāyana who belongs to a period earlier than that of Pānini. Uvat and Anantabhatta have written, respectively, Matriveda and Padārthiprakashaka to elucidate the Prātishākhya of Kātyāyana. Taittiriya Prātishākhya is related to Taittiriya Samhitā of Krishna Yajurveda. The commentary has been written by Mahishi, which is known as Padakramasadana.

Pushpasutra and *Riktantra* are the two Prātishākhyas on Sāmaveda. The author of *Pushpasutra* is supposed to be Vararuchi, and the author of *Riktantra* is supposed to be Shākatayāna.

Chaturādhyāyika is the oldest Prātishākhya of Atharvaveda. Kautsa is supposed to be the author of this Prātishākhya, which is also known as *Kautsa Vyākarana*.

The sixth Vedānga relates to jyotish,—astronomy and astrology. Jyotish is considered to be the science of light, and it is looked upon as the eyes among the Vedāngas. Vedic knowledge had discovered an inner rhythm of the cosmic movement, and this rhythm seems to correspond with periodic developments and seasons of human life. Time was conceived as succession of movements that measure growth, development and fulfilment of human aspirations. Since human aspirations and sacrifice were closely connected with each other, the determination of the time of the beginning and the end of sacrifices assumed a great importance. As a result, the transit of planets, calculation of days and nights and the determination of various seasons were closely studied. The science of Jyotish described planets, constellations, comets and also the rotations and revolutions of various luminous objects of the heavens. Corresponding to the movements of planets there were also predictions in regard to fortunate or unfortunate results in human life. This is at the root of astrology.

Rigveda Jyotish Vedānga has been attributed to Lagadhācharya. It consists of 36 verses. There is also Jyotish related to Yajurveda and another Jyotish related to Atharvaveda. Yajurveda Jyotish consists of 34 verses, and it has been attributed to Shoshāchārya. Atharvaveda Jyotish has 14 chapters and 102 verses. It is supposed to be a dialogue between Pitāmaha who was the speaker and Kashayapa who was the listener.

Among the greatest astronomers and astrologers of India, the most celebrated name is that of Varāhamihira. His famous book, *Pancha Siddhāntikā* speaks of 5 systems of Jyotish: Pitāmaha Siddhānta, Vasishtha Siddhānta, Romaka Siddhānta, Poulisha Siddhānta, and Surya Siddhānta. In due course, Jyotish inspired development of various sciences including arithmetic, algebra, geometry, astronomy and astrology. Bhaskarācharya of 12 century A.D. is regarded as the first among the mathematicians and astrologers of the middle ages. Jyotish is even today prevalent all over India, and it is even now a developing science. Panchānga, which gives detailed information regarding the tithi, vāra, nakshatra, yoga and karana, is commonly used in most of the Indian homes; and the annuals of Panchānga are constantly consulted by astronomers, astrologers and many individuals in the day-to-day life.

Apart from this Vedānga, there are also four other sciences and arts which have come to be known as Upavedas. The Upaveda of Rigveda is Āyurveda, the Upaveda of Yajurveda is Dhanurveda, the Upaveda of Sāmaveda is Gandharvaveda, and Upaveda of Atharvaveda is Arthaveda. Āyurveda is related to the secret of life and the science and art of sustenance, protection and maintenance of long life. The originator of Āyurveda is supposed to be Dhanwantari. Apart from him, other prominent names are Aitraeya, Kashyapa, Harit, Agnivesha, and Bhedamuni. At present, 3 important books of Āyurveda are: *Chakra Samhitā, Sushruta Samhitā,* and *Vāgbhatta Samhitā.* These three books are collectively called brihat-trayi.

Dhanurveda seems to be a very ancient science dealing with weapons of war and art of warfare. In the *Rāmāyana* and *Mahābhārata* a good deal of light is thrown upon this science and art, particularly in the descriptions of battles. The most ancient books of Dhanurveda are not available, but some of the known books are *Dhanurvidhi, Drauna Vidyā, Kodanda Mandana and Dhanurveda Samhitā*. According to the tradition, the originator of Dhanurveda is lord Shankara himself. Parashurāma is supposed to have learnt Dhanurveda from Lord Shankara. Dronācharya learnt this science from Parashurāma, and Arjuna learnt it from Dronācharya. Sattyaki is supposed to have learnt this science and art from Arjuna.

Gandharvaveda is the science of music, derived from Sāmaveda, and we have already dealt with this subject briefly, while dealing with the Vedānga of Chhanda.

Arthaveda is the Upaveda of Atharvaveda, which deals with social, economic, and political systems. It also deals with architecture and various arts. According to Shukranīti there are number of arts but 64 are considered to be more prominent. In later literature we find that 64 arts or Kalās were expected to be cultivated by a cultured lady. These included the art of cooking, skill in the use of body ointments and paints for the teeth, etc., music, dancing, painting, garland-making, floor decoration, preparation of the bed, proper use and care of dress and ornaments, sewing, elementary carpentry, repair of household tools and articles, reading, writing and understanding different languages, composing poems, understanding dramas, physical exercises, recreation from utilizing leisure hours, and the art of preparing toys for children.

The most famous book of Arthashastra is that of Kautilya. This book has remained authoritative, and many books which have been written thereafter on Arthashastra rely upon that book. Prior to Kautilya, we have also the famous enunciations of Bhishma and Vidura.

IV

For the proper understanding of the Veda, not only Vedangas but also itihāsa and purānas have been recommended. From the point of view of history (itihāsa), *Rāmāyana, Mahābhārata* and *Purānas* are consulted. But in Indian literature the word "itihāsa" refers mainly to *Mahābhārata*. Maharshi Valmiki is the author of *Rāmāyana* and *Mahābhārata* was composed by Maharshi Vedavyāsa. According to the tradition, the word Purāna is so-called because it is supposed to refer to the most ancient knowledge, even though the most ancient composition is that of the Veda. It is said that Brahmā had received the knowledge containing the Purānas from the Supreme Divine; Brahmā transmitted it to his four mind-born sons, including Sanat Kumāra. Narada received this knowledge from Sanat Kumāra, and he transmitted it to Krishna Dwaipāyana Vedavyāsa, Vedavyāsa composed that knowledge in 18 books, each one of them is called Purāna.

The names of these Puranas are given in the following table along with the number of verses mentioned against each:

Name	Number of verses
Brahma Purāṇa	10,000
Padma Purāṇa	55,000
Viṣṇu Purāṇa	23,000
Śiva Purāṇa	24,000
Bhāgavata Purāṇa	18,000
Nārada Purāṇa	25,000
Mārkaṇḍeya Purāṇa	25,000
Agni Purāṇa	10,500
Bhaviṣya Purāṇa	14,500
Brahmavaivarta Purāṇa	18,000
Liṅga Purāṇa	11,000
Varāha Purāṇa	24,000
Skanda Purāṇa	81,000
Vāmana Purāṇa	10,000
Kūrma Purāṇa	17,000
Matsya Purāṇa	14,000
Garuḍa Purāṇa	19,000
Brahmāṇḍa Purāṇa	12,000

There are also a number of Upapurānas, such as Narasimha, Nandi, Bhārgava, etc.

Purānas have been composed to explain the meanings of Vedas for common masses of people so as to evoke in them sensitivity in their being towards the Divine knowledge and to inspire in them devotion for the Supreme Reality. Purānas describe the creation of universe, development of universe, and the dissolution of the universe. In several Purānas, there is a good deal of description of the earth and its geography, and apart from many legends, there is also a description of secret knowledge relating to birth, death, and the condition of the soul after the death of the body. We also find in them questions and answers dealing with philosophic and yogic matters. Most importantly, Purānas are related to great deities, particularly Brahma, Vishnu, and Shiva. *Bhāgavata Purāna* is considered to be the most valuable book on Lord Krishna, and it is looked upon as an unparalleled composition on the theme of Shri Krishna and devotion to Shri Krishna. Purānas are also related to several other deities and great Rishis of the past. An important contribution of the Purāna is related to the concept of avatāra and the description of various avataras of the Supreme Divine.

Purāna literature is very vast and it has made a great impact on the religious and spiritual mind of India.

The tradition of philosophy in India goes back to very early times, and based upon the Veda, several systems of philosophy have flourished. These systems are: Nyāya, Vaisheshika, Sānkhya, Yoga, Poorva Mimāmsā and Uttara Mimāmsā. All these systems of philosophy accept the authority of the Veda, and although there are differences among them, attempts have also been made to bring about a synthesis of these systems of philosophy. The literature on these systems is to be found in the Sūtras attributed to great philosophers such as Gautama, Kanāda, Kapila, Patanjali, Jaimini and Bādarāyana, and in copious commentaries and commentaries on commentaries. In fact, even in the modern period there are expositions and commentaries on these systems of philosophy.

Bibliography

Altekar, A.S., *Education in Ancient India,* Banaras, 1951.

Dandekar, R.N., *Vedic Bibliography* (4 Vols.), Bhandarkar Oriental Research Institute, Poona.

Dasgupta, S.N., *A History of Indian Philosophy* (5 Vols.), Cambridge University Press.

Hastings. J., *Encyclopaedia of Religion and Ethics,* (13 Vols.), New York.

Hiriyanna, M., *Outlines of Indian Philosophy,* George Allen & Unwin, London.

Jayaswal, K.P., *Hindu Polity,* Calcutta, 1924.

Kunhan Raja, C., *The Vedas, A Cultural Study,* Andhra University, 1957.

Mira, *Veda Education in Ancient India,* Arya Book Depot, New Delhi, 1964.

Mother, The, *Mother's Agenda,* (Vol.2) Institut de Reserches Evolutives, Paris.

Mukherjee, Radha Kumud, *Ancient Indian Education,* London, Macmillan, 1951.

Radhakrishnan, S., *Indian Philosophy* (2 Vols.) George Allen & Unwin, London.

——— *Principal Upanishads,* George Allen & Unwin, London, 1953.

Renou, Louis, *Bibliographie Vedique,* Adrien Maisonneure, Paris, 1931.

Saraswati, Swamy Dayanand, *Satyartha Prakash,* Translated by Durga Prasad, Jan Gyan Prakashan, New Delhi, 1970.

Satprem, *The Revolt of the Earth,* Institute of Evolutionary Research, New York.

Sri Aurobindo, *The Secret of the Veda,* Sri Aurobindo Birth Centenary Library, Vol.10., Pondicherry.

——— *Hymns to the Mystic Fire,* Sri Aurobindo Birth Centenary Library, Vol.11, Pondicherry.

——— *The Upanishads,* Sri Aurobindo Birth Centenary Library, Vol.12, Pondicherry.

——— *The Foundations of Indian Culture,* Sri Aurobindo Birth Centenary Library, Vol.14, Pondicherry.

Thibaut, G., *Vedanta Sutras*, Sacred Books of the East, Oxford.

Varnekar, S.B., *Sanskrit Vangmaya Kosha* (2 vols.), Bhartiya Bhasha Parishad, Calcutta.

Vivekananda, Swami, *The Complete Works of Swami Vivekananda*, (8 Vols.), Advaita Ashrama, Calcutta.

Index